Forces of Nature

Nicholas Salaman was born in west Somerset, and educated at Radley and Oxford. He has written plays produced on television and the London stage, as well as a number of novels and children's books. He is married, lives in London, and plays the harpsichord.

NICHOLAS SALAMAN

FORCES OF NATURE

HarperCollins*Publishers*

HarperCollins*Publishers*
77–85 Fulham Palace Road,
Hammersmith, London W6 8JB

This paperback edition 1993
3 5 7 9 8 6 4 2

Previously published in paperback by Grafton 1990
Reprinted twice

First published in Great Britain by
The Alison Press/Martin Secker & Warburg Ltd 1989

Copyright © Nicholas Salaman 1989

The Author asserts the moral right to
be identified as the author of this work

ISBN 0 586 20785 6

Set in Times

Printed in Great Britain by
HarperCollinsManufacturing Glasgow

'. . . A huge peak, black and huge,
As if with voluntary power instinct,
Upraised its head.'

The Prelude – William Wordsworth

Preface

The action of Time, according to the best mathematical opinion, is to create disorder throughout a Universe that started in 'a very smooth and ordered state'. Everything that has happened subsequently has been a dissipation of energy at the expense of order.

If this is so, it is not perhaps as far-fetched as it might appear to seem in things that took place even thirty years or so ago, elements that reflect a fractionally more orderly world than the one we presently inhabit.

It may seem incredible now that parents could leave two boys of sixteen on their own for a fortnight at a remote guesthouse in one of the wilder and more inaccessible parts of England. Drug-pushers, perverts and child-murderers are only the most publicized of the dangers that have proliferated in the intervening years.

Of course there were violences and destructive wastes of energy then but it is arguable that they were more limited, just as an atom bomb is more limited than a hydrogen device.

We have come a long way, fast, since the Fifties. There has been a quantum leap, whatever that may be.

The limited violence of those times included the Korean and Malayan campaigns. The violence of the Second World War was only just behind. A sixteen-year-old boy knew that in two years he could be fighting. And if he had attended his School Corps (a more or less compulsory activity), he would be likely to find himself in a position of command, leading a platoon of thirty men or so into battle.

7

Initiative and self-sufficiency were the virtues propounded from a thousand school pulpits, and self-reliance was seen as the very antithesis of self-abuse.

So dropping boys in at the deep end was a regular and well-regarded aspect of their education.

This was the green and gold time when even the guilt seems, in retrospect, more innocent than today's. The whole decade of the Fifties was a sort of adolescence poised between the nitroglycerine and the nuclear ages. Popular television was still in its infancy. Ruby Murray was singing 'Softly, softly, come to me' and Eddie Calvert – the Man with the Golden Trumpet – was playing 'O mein Papa' all day long on the wireless. The Americanization of Britain had only just been thought of.

The attitude to sex deserves a passing mention since it has some bearing on the narrative. The condition today has swung back from the indiscriminate Babylon of the Sixties and Seventies to a climate of caution. Caution (for a very different reason) characterized carnal behaviour in the Fifties.

Sex in those days for the young was a dangerous mystery. A young man's chief dread was getting a girl pregnant – followed, some considerable way behind, by fear of the clap. Nice girls might well go to bed with you, but they simply did not give you gonorrhoea or syphilis. Non-specific urethritis had not been invented. As for herpes . . . cold sores stayed in places where you got colds.

There were crabs. But not in South Kensington.

There was ignorance about grownups among children and about children among grownups. Puberty was an awkward phase best ignored (it was much easier to do so if you sent your children to boarding school).

Teenage revolt had not yet been sanctified by James Dean.

The action in this story concerns events which occur in the North of England, a part of the country which was – and still is to some extent – wilder and more feudal than the softer South.

The lake Ettenwater is a combination of lakes, most of them in what is now called Cumbria.

If the present is a machine for turning the disorderly future into the past, it is as though certain loops and strands of time become caught up, and lie apart, exposed to the mind's eye, while new folds are buried under the endless spatter of the moment.

It is true, at any rate, of Fifties summers.

The smell of rain on country roads, and of water upon water; rare moments of pale sunlight reflected in fair hair; goat's milk; boathouse smells; all these renew themselves upon the senses as though indeed they were, and are, here now, always.

1

It was raining.

The road was as dark and shiny as the black pudding Freddie had seen someone eating for breakfast in the hotel near Matlock.

Freddie sat in the back of the Triumph Renown hedged in by pieces of luggage, and with his knee painfully nuzzled by a tennis racket press, and gazed at the fine reddish white hairs sprouting from the nape of his stepfather's neck.

His stepfather's name was Rollo. Freddie wrenched his eyes away from the neck.

They passed a signpost which said 'Windermere 8'.

'Funny thing about Windermere,' said Rollo. 'All the lavatories at school were called Windermere. Funny thing about Windermere. Windy sort of name.'

'We'll be at Ettenwater in twenty minutes,' said Freddie's mother brightly.

All the lavatories at Freddie's school were called Royal Flush but he didn't feel like talking to his stepfather very much. Instead he sat and glowered across at the French boy who sat almost hidden by bags and mackintoshes in the other half of the Triumph's back seat.

The French boy had the remains of tears still snailing down his face, but instead of feeling sorry for him, it made Freddie all the more furious. Why couldn't the weed show a bit more style? He was older than Freddie by six months. He'd been blubbing ever since he arrived.

Freddie's mother had explained that Bertrand had never been away from his family before, and that most boys in France didn't go to boarding school, but it hadn't encouraged Freddie's sympathy. Freddie had been sent to boarding school since the age of eight – although he had blubbed his eyes out at the time, he now knew it to be an indispensable part of English superiority.

'Have you stayed beside a lake, un lac, before?' asked Freddie's mother, relentlessly conversational.

'Ah, oui,' replied Bertrand miserably.

'Où?'

'Annecy.'

Bertrand started sniffing afresh at the memory of sweet sunshiny days with his mother and pretty sister.

'Oh yes, indeed. Such a beautiful lake. I remember going there before the war when . . .'

Freddie's mother prattled on while Freddie wondered how anyone could be so wilfully heedless of his wishes. His mother knew that he did not like the house filled with people during the school holidays, yet she persisted in doing it.

Au pair girls, paying guests, non-paying guests . . . they all made a bee-line for Marsh Barton House as though it were some kind of international study centre instead of being his home.

Not that home was all that wonderful or anything – set on the edge of a village in the orderly countryside of Bedfordshire – nothing much to do or many people to do it with. But he didn't need all these foreigners to share his mooching. They just made it worse.

His mother had a thing about foreigners. She believed in the brotherhood of nations and belonged to the English-Speaking Union.

His stepfather wasn't all that keen on the brotherhood of nations but he didn't mind the au pairs as long as they were pretty or made him laugh – preferably both. Besides, he had his den with the gramophone with the enormous

11

horn and his collection of records to retreat into. Freddie only had the dark bedroom at the top of the house and you didn't much feel like retreating up there unless you wanted a quick peep at *Men Only*. And even then you felt as if you were being sat on by the roof.

Typical of his mother to organize this holiday. Not that he'd had any very definite ideas on the subject himself, but anything would've been better than being landed with a French boy on Lake Ettenwater.

'It'll be a jolly good test of self-reliance,' his mother had said. 'It's good to be thrown in at the deep end.'

Knowing his dislike of company, his mother had set the thing up by stages.

'We're a bit short of money,' she had said to him when he had come home one Sunday from school, 'and my old friend Marie-Thérèse has asked if we will have her son Bertrand over as a p.g. sometime to get him to speak some English . . . It'll be nice for you to have someone to play with now Jamie's away . . .'

Jamie was Freddie's eighteen-year-old brother who had just gone off for National Service.

'I don't want to play with anyone. I'm sixteen. I'm happy on my own.'

'You can't play tennis on your own.'

It was one of his rare enthusiasms. Playing the piano – he had taught himself through reading music with the school choir – was another.

'I can play the piano on my own.'

'You must learn to be a bit more social, Freddie. Anyway, I think I'll see what she says. We'll see.'

Of course he should have known (not that he'd have been able to do anything about it). 'We'll see' was the way it always happened. No argument – just a fait accompli on his return for the holidays.

'But I said I didn't want anyone, Mother.'

'Well, he's coming now. I can't tell him to cancel all the arrangements. You'll just have to make the best of it.'

A little later, she had dropped the next bombshell. Freddie had asked at lunch whether they were going to Aldeburgh again for their holiday. His mother had looked at Rollo in a way which instantly aroused his suspicions.

'Well, Rollo and I have been invited to stay at Castle Coupar by Jock Coupar-Montrose . . .'

Rollo, though not well off himself, had a series of prosperous and titled relations. Freddie's mother, an engaging person of varied interests – she kept bees, watched birds and had a more than nodding acquaintance with all manner of wild flowers – was also a bit of a snob. She loved staying at castles and hobnobbing with the aristos.

Rollo was popular with his relations because he didn't appear often, never asked for money, and was mildly eccentric. He had the reputation of being a 'character'. Well into his fifties when he married Freddie's mother, he had seen many places, known many people. The fact that adolescent boys – especially Freddie – irritated him was not seen by the relatives as a disadvantage.

'Can I come?' asked Freddie.

'Well . . . we've got Bertrand coming . . .'

'Can't he come too, then?'

'Four's rather a lot for us to bring.'

'I gather they've got a houseful anyway. They haven't got room for any more. Not even a ewe lamb,' said Rollo, wandering around the lunch table and barging into Freddie as he reached over to put more peas on his plate. Ewe lamb was one of his stock jokes about Freddie. He was keen on stock jokes.

'But I didn't want the French boy in the first place,' said Freddie.

'Well, I've arranged a holiday for you so you won't

have to stay at home holding the fort with poor Hildegard.'

Hildegard was the current au pair from the Black Forest. She was eighteen and rather pretty in a snubby-faced way with shiny brown tresses and hairy armpits. She had once come into his room with cleaning things when he was reading *Esquire*. He didn't think she had seen.

'I wouldn't mind staying here with Hildegard.'

'Well, it wouldn't be convenient. I've booked up at the Flagg Foot Guest House now. We can drop you off on our way up to Castle Coupar and collect you on our way back.'

The enormity of the scheme was now striking home.

'You mean . . . a fortnight . . . with a French boy . . . who can't speak English . . . What'll we do?'

'Well, there's tennis . . . and boating . . . swimming and walking. Picnics . . . It'll be a challenge.'

'What if it rains?'

'I can't decide everything for you, Freddie. Show some gumption. Initiative . . .'

'I won't go.'

'Of course you will. You'll just have to grin and bear it.'

'Too bad,' said Rollo. 'It's just *too* bad.'

He was a messy eater. Fragments of pea and gravy clung to his chin in sufficient quantities (you'd have thought) to make their presence felt, but Rollo was too intent on mockery to be deflected by grease or crumb.

'Tooo baaad, Frap,' he neighed, using the semi-insulting acronym from Freddie's initials that he knew always made Freddie squirm; Frederick Randolph Army-tage Pemberton.

Freddie had prayed in the school chapel that Rollo would die as soon as he'd known that his mother was going to marry him. It wasn't that he was violent or

14

overtly cruel, but there was a sort of weak malice about him that was uncomfortable to live with. He always put a damper on your enthusiasms.

The fact that Rollo was still around after nearly four years of marriage had seriously eroded Freddie's belief in God.

However, it didn't stop him, on dull days – and there were plenty of those at Marsh Barton – dripping hour upon hour of Bedfordshire sempiternity when the seconds hung like the drops of moisture on the garden rhus bush – slowly picking out the tunes, and later the harmonies, of most of the hymns in Ancient and Modern and the English Hymnal.

He did this partly because he liked them and partly because he hoped Rollo would evince some gesture of appreciation – he longed for appreciation, even from Rollo. His stepfather would play Strauss and Mozart on the great horned gramophone every evening before dinner in his den, and was notorious for being fond of (particularly) light music – but doubtless because of this he detested Freddie's endless tinkling.

'What was that jejune little piece you were playing this morning?' he would occasionally enquire if he were in a good humour. 'I thought it particularly fatuous.'

And then he would refer to it again at supper with that high-pitched cackle more malicious now the whisky had got to work on it.

'Absolutely fatuous, Frap!'

But stubbornly Freddie continued to play. Half in the hope that one day he would play something so well that Rollo would be forced to compliment him. And half because he was becoming quite an authority on the hymnal. He could name the tune to just about any hymn you cared to mention, tell you who composed it and who

15

wrote the words, and often what number it was in the book.

It was a useless expertise – bolstered during termtime through Matins and Evensong sermons by having a chorister's hymnbook with music to leaf through, surreptitiously, while the preacher perorated.

Morning and evening, Easter and Advent, the very seasons of the year were measured in hymns – verses, tune names, composers, writers – 'Holy, Holy, Holy'; Melcombe; Bishop Ken; John Bacchus Dykes; 'Through all the changing scenes'; George Herbert; St Fulbert; Rockingham; the Executors of Mrs C. F. Alexander (why had she been executed?); Down Ampney; The Russian Contakion for the Departed; St Bees – words and four-part harmonies, all humming in his brain like bees in a church roof.

And now as they crossed the county boundary between Lancashire and Westmorland, the Pigling Bland boundary, it was 'Hills of the North, rejoice'. He looked round, half tempted to tell them, and then thought better of it.

His piano playing had progressed beyond hymns last term. Someone had given him an Early Classics Selection. Having been so schooled in the four-part progressions of the hymns, he now found he could play some of it: Bach, Handel, Couperin.

He started to hum a snatch of a Schubert waltz, hoping the French boy would be impressed at his sophistication.

'What's the matter, Frap? Indijaggers?' queried Rollo. 'All right back there?'

'Yes. Fine.'

'Thought I heard you groaning. It was you, wasn't it – not Bertrand? Bertrand . . .'

'Oui.'

'Grognez-vous?'

16

'Mais non.'

'There you are, you see. Must've been you, Frap.'

'I wasn't groaning. I was humming.'

'Mustn't groan if you're not sick. Otherwise when you really are groaning – say with acute ptomaine poisoning – we'll just think you're singing.'

Freddie wondered if Schubert had had a stepfather like Rollo, and, if so, what he would have composed for him.

'Only five more miles now, boys,' said Freddie's mother, who had gone into her usual optimistic trance while Rollo was teasing.

The full horror of the doom about to overtake him now dawned on Freddie.

Two weeks in a guesthouse in the rain with a wet French boy; two weeks out of his precious holidays. It was really too bad. His own tears – of indignation, frustration, loneliness – were close to the surface.

But suddenly they were crossing a little bridge over a pebbly river, huge hills loomed and the beginnings of a vast expanse of open water could be glimpsed between the trees.

Even in the rain – you could see the sploshing where the heavy drops hit the water, making huge Jeremy Fisher concentric circles – and in his mood of helpless hopelessness, Freddie was momentarily impressed.

It really was a great deal of lake. It made Bedfordshire seem a bit tame – and at the same time infinitely reassuring.

'Regarde, Bertrand. Le lac d'Ettenwater,' said his mother, pronouncing it 'Ettenvorter' which she said was the French way with a w.

Bertrand stared out miserably as if it were the stream of Acheron.

'Ah, oui,' he said.

17

'C'est long d'une douzaine de milles,' she went on. 'C'est à dire, presque vingt kilomètres.'

'Ah, oui,' said Bertrand.

Was that all he would say? Was that all he was ever going to say? Ah oui, ah oui.

'Gosh, that's really long,' said Freddie, in the midst of his misery suddenly sorry for his mother.

Really, the frog didn't have to be quite such a vet blanket. This fluctuation between impatience and protectiveness towards his mother had already become a source of tension in his life. At least, he told himself, for two weeks he wouldn't have to feel embarrassed when she laughed too loud. It didn't comfort him much.

He wished his friend Aitken was here instead of the French boy, and he could tell him about his vet blanket joke. On the other hand, if the French boy wasn't around, there wouldn't be any joke to tell . . .

The road now started to climb among rocky hillocks and a little wood above the right-hand shore of the lake. Through the rain he could see a huddle of grey stone buildings on the opposite shore. The cloud was low on the hillside beyond. A few sheep mooched about glumly in the dampness. There was no sign of humanity.

'Look, boats, boys. You'll be able to hire a boat from there.'

There was indeed a little landing stage and a flotilla of waterlogged skiffs.

'"Jolly boating weather,"' said Rollo.

'Ah oui,' said Bertrand.

'That'll do, Rollo. We're nearly there,' said Freddie's mother, as they turned a corner and saw another huddle of buildings on the shore below them, lapped by the lake. 'Look. That must be it. Yes, there's the sign. Flagg Foot . . .' In faded lettering it announced, Flagg Foot Guest House, Board and Accommodation.

'Flat Foot,' quipped Rollo, turning off the road into the drive. 'Hullo . . . goats! You're going to be quaffing goat's milk, Frap.'

A little herd of the creatures were waiting patiently outside a barn. Freddie shuddered. Rollo knew his horror of the distinctive taste of goat.

'I won't be able to drink it, Mother,' he said, panicking. 'It tastes of sweat.'

'Goat's milk is a great delicacy in France,' said his mother. 'N'est-ce pas, Bertrand? Chèvre?'

'Ah oui.'

'Anyway darling, I'm sure they'll have cow's milk too.'

The car scrunched to a stop outside the front door. Rollo was a clumsy driver – and Freddie could see them already earning black marks from the guesthouse proprietor for digging into his gravel.

Rollo switched the engine off and the windscreen wipers stopped. The car started to steam up and fat raindrops waddled across the windscreen.

2

'This is my son Freddie, Mr Aylott,' Freddie's mother enthused, 'and this is Bertrand who lives in Paris. His grandmother was an old school friend of my mother's.' As she prattled unnecessarily on, Freddie took stock of the landlord.

Aylott was a thin bespectacled abstracted-looking fellow in his forties, Freddie guessed. School had given him a good instinct for older men. He decided that Aylott was going to be a negative to neutral influence. His air of embittered abstraction was probably due to the matter of trying to make his guesthouse pay in a wet summer. But while it was good from the point of view of non-intervention, it also meant that there was going to be no cosy father-substituting figure to take them for runs in the car or teach them fly-fishing, or whatever it was that father substitutes did and Rollo most assuredly didn't.

Mrs Aylott now made an appearance, smoothing her palms on an apron.

She shook hands and bolted back towards the kitchen. Her general demeanour was much as that of her husband with perhaps an added ingredient of watchfulness – although it could have been something to do with whatever was cooking behind the kitchen door.

'Would you like to see the lads' room?' Aylott asked Freddie's mother.

'If we might.'

Freddie's mother put on her most irritating don't-want-to-be-a-nuisance face, a sort of keen puzzled trusting expression, and pointed it at Mr Aylott's back as he led them down a pine-panelled floor-sealed corridor on the ground floor which turned abruptly – first to the left and then to the right. It seemed for the size of the place an inordinately long walk.

'We don't want to be too long, darling,' said Rollo, having misgivings about arriving in Scotland too late for the gins and tonics.

'Here we are,' said Aylott, throwing open the door. 'I reckon you'll find yourselves pretty comfortable in here.'

With a horrible start of shock and dismay Freddie realized the appalling truth. They were going to make him share a room with the frog. No, this was too much. It was time to put his foot down.

Hardly bothering to look around the room – a pine-clad chamber with two beds, two chairs, two chests of drawers and one cupboard, commanding a view of a sloping field with the goathouse at one end and a sliver of lake at the other – he cleared his throat. His mother turned to him, gaily.

'Isn't it lovely, Freddie? With a view of the lake as well! C'est joli, n'est-ce pas, Bertrand?'

'Ah oui.'

'I er just didn't realize I'd be sharing a room.'

'Oh but surely it's jollier to share?'

She knew that Freddie valued his privacy but she regarded the foible as anti-social.

'Well, it's just . . . I might want to read when Bertrand wants to sleep.'

'Oh well . . . look . . . you have your own bedside lights. You wouldn't mind him reading, would you, Bertrand? Il veut lire quelquefois. Ça ne vous dérangera pas, hein?'

'Ah non.'

Freddie was summoning up all his stubbornness when Aylott put the kibosh on it.

'I'm afraid we didn't have two single rooms suitable, Mrs Lanchester. And of course in t'figures we discussed . . .'

'Of course. Freddie doesn't mind, do you, Freddie?'

'Frap doesn't mind. And even if he does it's just too bad. Toooo baaad, Frap,' said Rollo. 'Beatie, time to go.'

There was nothing Freddie could do about it. He could feel the tears welling up again and turned as if to look at the view. A billy goat was busily mounting a nanny over by the water's edge while the nanny continued her meal of nettles. The billy goat dismounted and looked round disgustedly as the grownups went back down the corridor, almost as if he'd been laying it on for their delectation. The boys lingered by the window. Freddie toyed with the idea of making a joke about 'laying it on' but he didn't know the right French. Anyway he knew what the French boy would have replied.

'Ah oui.'

'Come along, Beatie,' said Rollo in the driveway. 'Say goodbye to your eewee lamb.'

'Goodbye, darling,' said his mother. 'Have a lovely time and look after Bertrand. You've got our telephone number. And don't forget to look up the Seathwaites. Mr Aylott will show you where they live. I wish I could remember, there was some funny story about them, made us all laugh. Cousin Percy, you know, the archaeologist . . .'

'Perky the Arseologist,' chipped in Rollo.

'Percy the Archaeologist,' said his mother for the benefit of Bertrand, though she usually laughed at the joke, 'he met someone who'd stayed there. No, I simply can't remember. Never mind. I expect it'll come back. Goodbye, darling. Goodbye, Bertrand. Au revoir . . .'

The two boys watched as the car chewed its way across the gravel and retreated up the drive until it was hidden by the shadowy trees near the gate; and then, without speaking to each other, they trudged back across the Welcome mat into the gravy-laden imponderabilities of the guesthouse.

3

It was inevitable that they should find there was nothing to do in Flat Foot.

It was true there was a small Res Lounge (that was what it said on the door), but it only contained a few out-of-date copies of *Country Life* and some packs of playing cards. Freddie hated cards anyway – Rollo was a devotee of bridge – so he wasn't much mortified by the discovery that the packs were incomplete. There were a couple of perished ping-pong bats but no sign of ball or table, and when he went back to ask about them, the Aylotts seemed to have disappeared. He didn't like to go into the kitchen.

Bertrand muttered something in French and retreated down the corridor to the lavatory. Freddie turned his attention to a local newspaper, the *Lakeland Clarion*, whose date was somewhat more recent than the other publications. It was only two months old. Across the front page, it said: 'Monster sighting in Ettenwater'.

Here was the first interesting thing about the place. He read on: 'Manchester businessman Arthur Bembow and his wife stopped for a romantic lakeside drink. The light was just beginning to fade when, says Arthur, "We saw a swirling movement in the water over towards the eastern shore. It grew bigger and started to move rapidly in our direction. When it reached the middle of the lake, we could see that there was something rising up from the wave. My wife and I became alarmed and hastily gathered up our things, leaving a much valued Thermos flask, luckily insured. From a standing position, we could see

there was a dark hump-like object causing the wash, which now reared up followed by another hump, and finally a blunt snout-like head. The creature seemed to measure at least 40 feet. It gazed about in a puzzled manner and, finally, when it was no more than 200 yards from our position, it plunged once more into the depths."
Mr Bembow and his wife were staying at the Flagg Foot Guest House. This is not the first time that a creature has been seen in the lake. Indeed Wordsworth himself was said to have seen huge shapes. But the sightings have been rare . . .'

Freddie became aware that there was somebody else in the room. He turned and saw it was the worried-looking wife of the proprietor.

'Everything all right?' she enquired. 'Very pleased to have you, I'm sure. Very pleased. Room all right, to your satisfaction? Good.'

It was most obliging of her, thought Freddie, to answer her questions for you. It dispensed with a great deal of useless dialogue.

'Breakfast from eight-thirty to nine,' she went on, 'and we serve high tea from six o'clock to six-thirty. Will that suit you? So glad. Anything else you'd like to know?'

Freddie jumped in before she could reply this time.

'The monster?' he asked. 'Is there one in the lake? It says here . . .'

He pointed at the newspaper.

Mrs Aylott paused for a moment. He thought he detected a certain evasiveness or craftiness in her eyes, but it could have been the stuffed trout on the chimney-piece reflecting in her glasses. Mr Aylott's voice interrupted from the doorway.

'That were all a lot of hocus-pocus, that were. Them two were staying here. All Wordsworth and wisdom of the universe. Weird and wonderful. I reckon they'd been drinking. They had gin and ice in that there Thermos. We've lived here for ten years and we never heard of a monster. Course there's folk will talk. And there's some will lead 'em on. But Ettenwater isn't Loch Ness and never will be.'

'Oh,' said Freddie, disappointedly.

'Now, young feller,' said Aylott, 'I told your mother that I'd keep an eye on you. But I'm busy 'enough as it is so I'll just spell out a few – I won't call 'em rules – recommendations more like, but you'll see as how they make sense. The lake is deep and cold, and we're near the deep end. So watch out if you go swimming. It's colder than you think. Then there are funny currents. Don't know about monsters but we have had drownings here – one only last month. Things to do. There's a place that hires boats out across the bridge but don't lark about and fall in. If you do, and you're far out, that could be your come-uppance or should I say go-downance. Tell your pal, won't you? Mrs Aylott and I are mono-lingual. Walking: walk where you like but take a map – know how to read a map? – and look out for the mist on the fells. I've known people never come down . . .'

Mr Aylott paused. Freddie's lively imagination was a great source of nervousness to him. It looked as if this place were a kind of all-purpose death-trap.

'Right, lad. That's all for the moment. Use your initiative and keep your nose clean, and you won't go far wrong. Rain's stopping if I'm not mistaken. Take a shufti before tea, spot a monster, ho ho ho, might see a fish jump. Six o'clock sharp, don't forget. Mrs Aylott doesn't like to be kept waiting.'

Mrs Aylott gave a blink to show her potential ire, and the two of them went back towards the kitchen.

Freddie nearly went out by himself – his wellingtons had been put in a stand in the porch – but a sort of half-politeness made him go back to the room to see if the French boy had emerged. It was the last thing he, Freddie, needed. Nothing but Ah-wee-wee-wee wherever they went, whatever they looked at. But his mother's sociability was strong and – because he was missing her – he did the decent thing.

Opening the door of their bedroom, he found Bertrand unpacking. He had put a photograph of a woman on the table beside his bed. Freddie walked over – somehow you needed to be close up when talking French – and was about to speak when his eye was caught by the fact that the woman in the photograph was rather beautiful. He looked at the boy again. Yes, there was a definite similarity.

'Ma mère,' said Bertrand, moistly.

'Elle est belle,' said Freddie.

'Ah oui,' said Bertrand and burst into tears.

Freddie had spent much time in the dormitory at school speculating with the others on the charms of young ladies. A magazine called *Health and Efficiency* in which Swedish women with breasts like Bofors reclined against trees and rocks was circulated, much-thumbed, and embellished with other indefinable stains. Those who had got a pass into Oxford for an afternoon would sometimes come back with French letters purchased at the surgical store in St Peter's Street. These would be shown round and carefully hoarded against the day when they might be pressed into action. No one had actually slept with a woman yet, though Hibbert said his sister had shown him her cunt and it didn't look up to much. Aitken had a bet going that he would be the first.

Some of the boys had what were known as 'little men' – younger boys of thirteen or so, usually in their first year – who looked like girls, and who were sometimes cuddled in classroom cupboards or up in School Wood.

Freddie himself had gone into a cupboard once or twice, but he somehow thought it would be infinitely nicer with a girl. The trouble was, being brought up mainly by women, that he had somehow got the idea that girls were 'better', purer creatures than boys – so it would be difficult to think of oneself being dirty with them.

It was confusing. Freddie wondered whether Bertrand felt confused too but it was a difficult matter to go into with an only limited grasp of declensions. Besides, the youth was blubbing. Embarrassed, he half put an arm on his shoulder.

'Voulez-vous voir les environs?' he asked, conscious of the gap between his gesture and the stilted enquiry.

Bertrand put his hand up and clutched him mutely. They stood there for a moment. Freddie felt both embarrassed and yet oddly sympathetic. He was glad Aitken couldn't see him like this.

It was good about the monster, though, even if it didn't exist.

4

The view up the lake from Flat Foot's little landing stage was at the same time impressive and dejecting. The water stretched in a widening swathe from the narrow point where they stood into an illimitable distance, and its whole surface seemed to leap and quiver with liquidity as if in some kind of multiple conjugative fandango with the rain.

The boys stood there looking hopelessly out onto the water, each locked in his own private misery, as the downpour hissed and slithered over their wellingtons.

Freddie recalled that Beatrix Potter had written Jeremy Fisher somewhere near here, doubtless after just such a watery afternoon, but it seemed hardly polite to draw the froggy's attention to the fact. Instead he pointed at the grey stone buildings they could see about a mile away towards the extreme southern end of the lake, up on the farther side.

'Let's go over and have a look,' he said. 'Regardons là.'

Bertrand fell in beside him, but they had barely walked a dozen paces when a distant, extraordinary, dull bellowing diverted their attention. It seemed to be coming from further up the lake to their right, where they could just discern a stone building in the distance, half hidden in a wooded gully.

By common accord, the two boys changed direction and made across the meadow to trace the source of the sound, Freddie checking nervously for rams. Approaching the end of the first field, they were momentarily put off by the sight of a padlocked gate into the next and a notice which said 'PRIVATE – KEEP OUT – CHIEN MECHANT'.

'Ah, chien méchant,' said Bertrand. 'Notty dog.'

It was the first English Freddie could remember hearing him speak, and it deflected his attention from the anomaly of a French notice in an English field.

'I don't like notty dogs much,' he confided.

'Ni moi n'en plus,' said Bertrand.

It was the first time Freddie had seen even so much as a hint of a smile upon his face.

Suddenly the air was filled once more with the baleful roaring.

'C'est pas un chien,' said Freddie decisively.

The roar was more like a minotaur with a twisted jockstrap than any earthly hound.

'Venez donc,' said Bertrand.

It was too extraordinary to be resisted, and yet perhaps after all it was a bull, Freddie decided. He had had one nasty encounter as a child in a mushroom field. At the same time, he did not like to see the French boy take the honours in valour (even if it were due to ignorance of social conditions). He was saved by the bell – or rather the gong from Flat Foot, sounding tremulously across the meadows calling the faithful to high tea.

'Peut-être il faut que nous retournions,' he said, in a fuddle of reflexives and subjunctives. But the weedy froggy seemed to be made of sterner stuff.

'Non, non,' he said. 'En avant.'

'We'd better go back for high tea, le thé en haut,' said Freddie. 'We don't want to be late. C'est nécessaire pour la première fois, au moins, que nous sommes pas en retard.'

'Le thé en haut? We go upstairs for the tea?'

'Le thé et les baked beans et le pain frit et un pichet de

lait à chèvre,' said Freddie in a burst of conversational confidence. 'High tea, comprenez? Not upstairs. High tea à l'anglais.'

'Oof,' said Bertrand, wincing.

5

It is difficult to discuss a bizarre sound or indeed a bizarre anything when drinking tea made with goat's milk. The combination of the familiar and the disgusting pushes speculation – especially in French – to the back of the palate.

While Bertrand wrestled with the baked beans on greasy fried bread (Freddie's prognosis had proved only too accurate), their temporary rapport almost seemed never to have taken place.

The boy was sunk once again in impenetrable melancholy. It was the end of a long day, and the effect which English guesthouse cooking has on the Parisian was taking its inevitable toll. But Freddie was not at an age when making allowances comes easily. He was irrationally beginning to feel insulted by Bertrand's attitude to Flat Foot food. After all, it was no worse than school.

They were the only people in the dining room. The rain had kept the passing trade late or at home – Freddie later discovered that few people actually stayed more than a night at Flat Foot, which served as an inconvenient staging post from industrial Lancashire – moisture even seemed to have got into the baked beans, which sloshed about in a meagre sauce.

They were served by an impudent girl of about twelve who, it became clear, had taken an overwhelming fancy to the French youth.

'Ooo, I do like him, I really do,' she said to Freddie after she had failed to engage Bertrand in conversation. 'I really really really do.'

Her stripling breasts positively bristled with excitement. It was the first time that Freddie had become aware of the ranker side of female passion.

'I wet my knickers for him,' she said. 'You tell him.'

'Please,' said Freddie, still hungry and trying to decide whether to have cornflakes for pudding. The milk was bad enough without all this extra goatishness.

And secretly he was rather hurt that the girl preferred Bertrand to himself. He had complained to his mother that he wasn't as good-looking as he would have liked and she had assured him that girls value other things. Here was direct refutation.

'And if I tempted am to sin
And outward things are strong
Do thou, O Lord, keep watch within
And guard my soul from wrong,'

he admonished her.

'Stuck up little turd,' she told him, tartly.

'Elle dit qu'elle a mouillé ses pantalons pour vous,' said Freddie.

'Ah oui?' said Bertrand.

'Come out at once and don't linger with the guests,' said Mrs Aylott, appearing at last, wiping an eternal wisp of hair from her eye, 'or I'll fetch you such a thump. My niece,' she explained, 'up here for a few days to help me out. Just send her packing, she's nothing but trouble. Whatever do they teach them at school?'

The girl grinned and slipped away.

'We heard a rather funny noise,' he said to Mrs Aylott.

'Oh yes?'

'It was a sort of groaning sound. Like a sort of bullock. Further up by the lake.'

'Oh, that's who we call the Commander,' she said. 'He's got all sorts of instruments down at his boathouse. And that's not all he's got,' she added cryptically.

33

'Instruments?' asked Freddie.

'Well, he's nautical, isn't he?' said Mrs Aylott, vaguely, and scuttled off as Mr Aylott's variant of ululation came from the kitchen.

There seemed to be a lot of bellowing round these parts, thought Freddie, wanting to discuss the matter with someone but baffled by the language barrier.

Ingeminatus was the Latin for a bellow, but he couldn't remember the French. It made him irritated with the boy all over again.

'Bellow,' he said. 'Qu'est-ce que c'est bellow en français?'

'Sais pas.' A French shrug.

'Grogner?'

'Vous voulez grogner encore?'

'Je veux pas grogner. But I bally will grogner if you don't start talking some English soon.'

'Quoi? Pardon.'

Freddie could have thrown his cornflakes, goat's milk and all, over the youth in his frustration.

But later in the bedroom, when they had cleaned their teeth and the French boy had said his prayers, after undressing chastely behind the cupboard door because he hadn't been to boarding school, and Freddie said a prayer too because he didn't want to be shown up to God by a Catholic, and they had got into their beds and turned the lights out, and lay listening to the liquid darkness, Freddie couldn't help feeling sorry for him again as the sniffles turned into sobs.

The boy sounded so utterly desolate that Freddie in the end got up and went over to him, intending to say a comforting word and bestow a helpful pat on the head. But the bedclothes suddenly erupted and the boy flung himself into his arms where he lay weeping and groaning and ingeminating in the most piteous manner.

34

Freddie waited half embarrassed, half curiously flattered, until the boy seemed asleep, and finally padded back to his own bed.

The next thing he was conscious of was a monumental wet dream in which a Cumberland sausage, the precocious waitress and Bertrand's beautiful mother were all inextricably woven.

As he woke up, for a terrible moment he thought he was still in Bertrand's bed, coming interminably onto Bertrand's blue poplin pyjama bottoms.

He started to babble apologies in French, but mercifully, he now saw, the bed was his own as indeed were the pyjamas.

Freddie switched on his bedside light. Bertrand seemed asleep. His angelic head turned sideways on the pillow and a half-smile on his face. Freddie dabbed at himself ineffectually, fearful of waking him up, and switched off the light again.

Had Bertrand heard? What would he think about the patch on his pyjamas? (He might do some judicious sponging in the morning.) Had there been, moving in and out of the dream, Bertrand's own face as well?

Freddie fell asleep, borne on the comfortable tide of lust innocently fulfilled. Even a monk couldn't help it, Aitken said.

6

They were woken up, horribly early, by a banging at the door.

Before Freddie even had time to collect his wits or make any kind of response, the handle turned and the door flew open.

It was the small girl carrying a tray upon which slopped two teacups.

'Bonjour, I'm Isobel,' she said. 'I forgot to tell you. But they call me Jezebel at school. You can call me Fifi, chéri,' she continued to Bertrand, who was trying to believe he might still be at home in his mother's comfortably modish little flat near the Bois de Boulogne.

'Ooof,' he said, turning over and pulling the bedclothes over his head.

'Voulez vous coucher avec moi?'

'Look,' said Freddie, 'I don't want to be rude, but don't you think it's a bit early for all that? I mean, you're a bit young, aren't you? And what time is it, anyway?'

'It's twenty to eight and I'm thirteen,' she replied, not in the least abashed. 'Breakfast's at half past so move your butt.'

Where did the child pick up her language? It was riper than a Colt's cricket box.

'My father was a GI,' she said as if reading his thoughts, 'but Mum missed home so we had to come back, worse luck. I hate this crummy country.'

'Thank you,' said Freddie, feeling that the conversation had reached the end of any possible use. 'Tea, Bertrand? Thé de bonne heure du matin?'

'Merci,' said the French boy, muffledly.

'That means he *doesn't* want it,' said Freddie.

'Yes, he does.'

'Just put it down here, and wend.'

'Wend?'

'Your way.'

It was a favourite dismissal at school but it didn't seem to have the desired effect on Jezebel. She sat down on his bed and scratched her leg ruminatively.

'Tell me,' she said. 'What's it like being a boy? I mean, d'you jerk off a lot?'

In the light of last night's activities, Freddie found this a specially unwelcome topic, but masturbation, at any time, was a knotty subject. The Headmaster occasionally gave little talks urging the boys not to 'tamper with the springs of life', though whether it was your own springs or somebody else's springs he did not exactly impart. There were rumours that excessive masturbation – or masterbasshion as the Head pronounced it, pouting his lips priestlily around the consonant – was bad for your vision or could bring on convulsions. A boy called Catto was known to have given himself a hernia from 'moving in the bed'. No one seemed to have a good word for it.

But in spite of all the warning, there was scarcely a day when the notion did not present itself.

God, of course, viewed it gravely. He knew that. The Chaplain said so, and anyone could see that Love Divine all loves excelling would have nothing in common with pocket billiards and a copy of *Titbits* or *Amorous Adventures of a Gentleman of Leisure* under the desk at prep.

It was indeed a vexed area and one which he frequently returned to. Erections could suddenly appear like squalls out of an innocent-seeming sky. He had had them while doing press-ups in the Gym; in his swimming trunks lying in hot sun; at the Madrigal Society looking at Lulu, the

Housemaster's daughter, while singing 'April is in my Mistress' face'; in Chapel opposite Peters whom you'd boasted to Aitken you were keen on and wanted as your 'little man', and Aitken had told the whole of the rest of the dormitory. Car and bus journeys were particularly fraught, and he had once helplessly come under a copy of *Picture Post* on a train journey in the same compartment as a missionary.

Aitken had thought that exquisitely funny.

'Emissionary,' he cackled, falling about in the Long Corridor.

In spite of all this interesting material, Freddie did not now see why this little squirt of a girl should be privy to his innermost ebbs and flows.

'I don't jerk at all,' he said, 'not that it's any of your business. I had my parts chewed off by a dog when I was a baby.'

But even that didn't deflect her.

'Ooo. Let's see.'

'Look. Fuck off, will you.'

He held tightly onto the sheet fearful that she would spot the stain on his pyjama bottoms.

It was the first time he had ever used such rank language on a girl, but he couldn't help feeling it was justified, and he was pleased to notice that it seemed to have effect. She stuck her tongue out at him and retreated up the corridor without closing the door.

'I'll tell my auntie of you,' she said.

Freddie was momentarily alarmed. What would he and the froggy do if they were turned out? Where would they go? He had a little money but it was only for entertainment, not for living on.

'Qu'est-ce que c'est que fuck-off?' enquired Bertrand.

'C'est à dire allez-vous-en.'

'Ah oui.'

A fine rain was falling. Outside, the trees clumped in little fuddles of moisture. The boys brushed their teeth and dressed in silence, Freddie keeping his pyjamas to the wall, Bertrand dressing chastely behind the opened cupboard. The lino on the floor was damp. Freddie began to wish he were at school again – a thing he had never ever done in the holidays. God knew what the French youth was thinking; wishing he were on Devil's Island, most likely.

A gong sounded up the corridor.

'Venez donc, Bertrand,' said Freddie, and they padded hopelessly up the corridor in Indian file towards the dining room.

A fat man with over-black hair parted down the middle was seated at a table near the window eating cornflakes with embarrassingly loud percussions. Freddie was appalled to see that the only other table laid was next to him. He looked like the sort of person who would want to talk.

'Morning,' said the man, as they drew up their chairs.

'Good morning,' said Freddie.

'Goat's milk,' said the man, sloshing it on the flakes. 'Can't beat it. That's why I come here. I come here for the goat's milk. Marvellous.'

Freddie shuddered. He didn't feel in any way able to reply.

'Cat got your mouth, has it?'

'Sorry?'

'Sorry,' the man minced. 'Too stuck up to talk? This is the North, y'know.'

'I know.'

'Of course, you know. You're at school. That's what schools are for. Know when I left school, know-all?'

Freddie wanted to be anywhere but here and shifted uneasily on his seat. There was something on it which was sticking to his trousers. It seemed to have the consistency of half-dry semen. Bertrand stared fixedly out of the window as if the rain were some kind of accident.

'I left school when I were younger than you. And look at me now. Travel in lingerie. Not underwear. Lingerie. Don't forget that. I'll give you a peek after.'

Mrs Aylott came in with a notebook.

'Good morning,' she said evasively.

Freddie thought perhaps she had troubles of her own. There was a slight air of sadness about her, so maybe she didn't mean to be so evasive after all. At least the girl hadn't spilled the beans about his bad language.

'Good morning,' he said.

Suddenly he was furious with Bertrand. Why wouldn't the little weed at least say good morning too? Surely even the French understood good manners?

'There's cornflakes or grapefruit segments,' she began but the fat man interrupted.

'Take the cornflakes. They're fantastic with the goat's milk. Fantastic.'

He pronounced it funtastic.

'Let the boys make up their own minds, Mr Leacock.'

He would be called Leacock, thought Freddie.

'And to follow, there's fried egg, bacon 'n tomato. All right?'

'Take the fried egg,' said Mr Leacock.

'I'll have the grapefruit segments, please. Et vous, Bertrand? Les cornflakes ou la . . .' he couldn't think of the word for grapefruit.

'Oo la la,' said Mr Leacock. 'Your friend French, is he? Wait till he sees my French knickers, he'll go ape. Take him right back to Gay Paree. I'll tell you that for starters.'

'You mustn't mind Mr Leacock,' said Mrs Aylott. 'He's one of my regulars.'

40

'That's right, like Eno's Salts, lads. Just passing through. I wear many hats.'

'Pamplemousse,' said Freddie with a huge effort of memory. He wanted more than anything in the world to get out of here.

'Non,' said Bertrand, not helping at all.

'The cornflakes, then?' said Mrs Aylott.

'Non. Rien pour moi.'

'Give him the pamplemousse,' said Freddie. 'If he doesn't want it, I'll have it.'

Bertrand did not eat the grapefruit, or the greasy egg and bacon or the soggy toast. He took one taste of the goat's milk tea and spat it back in a cup.

'That lad's got a touch of nostalgia,' said Mr Leacock, observing their every action as if he were fattening them for Christmas. 'I know what he needs. Here you are, lad. This'll cheer you up.'

And he delved into a case which he had secreted under his table and waved a pair of silky drawers at the French adolescent.

'There,' he said to Freddie, 'for your nancy boy. If he don't want to wear them himself he can give 'em to his mother. Pour ta mère,' he repeated bullyingly.

The French boy took the knickers, regarded them gravely, opened the window and threw them out into the rain. Windows seemed to bring out the best in him, thought Freddie.

Mr Leacock's face was a picture.

'Well,' he said at length, 'well, I don't know about that. Best quality rayon they were. He'll have to pay.'

'But you gave them to him, Mr Leacock,' said Freddie.

'Not to throw out into the rain, si'thee.'

'Giving's giving,' said Freddie, definitely. They were very hot at that sort of thing at school. 'I'll get them if

41

you like though. Dry them in our room and give them to some deserving case.'

'Eh well, then, cut along,' said Mr Leacock. 'Best gather 'em up before Aylott happens on 'em. Drawers in the driveway is not the best advert for a family guesthouse.'

As luck would have it, of course, returning to their room with the sodden knickers held fastidiously in front of him, Freddie was spotted by the obnoxious Isobel. She burst into peels of laughter.

'Well, fuck me,' she said, 'you've started early. Who did you whip those off?'

With some dignity, Freddie explained what had happened. Isobel was not impressed.

'A likely tale,' she said. 'But I'll give you the benefit of the doubt if you hand 'em over to me. I might be able to find a home for them.'

'Aren't you a little young for French knickers?'

'If you're big enough, you're old enough.'

'But you're not big enough.'

'Like to look? How d'you fancy a kick in the balls?'

There was no arguing with the child. Freddie tried another tack.

'Anyway, they belong to Bertrand.'

'Voulez vous me donner le slip?' she asked the youth. 'Mon corps s'est enragé d'envie de ça.'

'Ah oui,' said the French boy.

'Where did you learn French?' asked Freddie.

'My father was stationed at Fontainebleau. He was a menial jerk,' said the girl.

7

It was still raining after breakfast – rather harder if anything.

Bertrand said he wanted to write a lettre, and shut himself up in the bedroom covering sheets and sheets of notepaper in a sloping Gallic scrawl which Freddie had a quick peep at when he heard him go off to the lav.

He feared he might be telling his family what an awful time he was having, but the letter seemed to contain nothing worse than accounts of the English food, the topography of the lake, and declarations of affection. How he could cover so much paper and say so little was a mystery of the same order as those endless jabber-jabber-jabbers of stout women on continental buses.

The first half of Freddie's own morning was spent in the Res Lounge trying to read *The Prelude*.

That had been another of his mother's excuses to send him up here – his A Levels. *The Prelude* Books 1 and 2 was one of the set texts in the English Literature exam. It was a bit steep. He'd only just finished his O Levels. But his mother was the daughter of a don, and regarded the acquisition of learning as others view the accumulation of capital.

Clearly the weather in Wordsworth's day had been an improvement on the current summer. It made Freddie grit his teeth to read about the precocious youth's curriculum:

'In a small mill-race severed from his stream,
Made one long bathing of a summer's day;

43

Basked in the sun, and plunged and basked again
Alternate, all a summer's day, or scoured
   The sandy fields, leaping through flowery groves . . .'

Wordsworth wouldn't be leaping through flowery
groves with the rain peeing down as it was today. He
would be sploshing through flowery groves with water in
his gumboots; but doubtless that wouldn't have sounded
so good in the textbooks.

He couldn't help feeling that Wordsworth was a pill
with a rose-tinted memory.

Finally, he gave up and turned his attention to the only
book of any interest on the shelves, an ancient volume
called *Roving Through Lakeland* published in 1863.

He turned the pages until he came to Ettenwater.
Skipping through lavish descriptions of the paths across
the fells from Coniston (the author, a certain Ashley
Merewether, had obviously sipped at the same fount as
Wordsworth since he was constantly hie-ing and hither-
ing), he paused at a section headed Legends and Local
Lore.

'Ettenwater' he read, 'is a wild and sequestered lake
around which few proper settlements have ever been
made. Around its north-eastern side, the lower slopes of
Stickletop slide headlong into the water in a cataract of
scree and debris as though this place has been the scene
of some titanic struggle in days of yore – or indeed a
geological cataclysm halted in its course only by Almighty
command which, once revoked, will send the whole
mountainside hurtling downwards again. Towards the
southern end, it is true, a more gentle mien may greet the
traveller, but it is deceptive, for the shallows here soon
give way to great depths, and the water is at all times
cruelly cold. Whether the lake is truly bottomless, and
leads to one of the portals of the Underworld as local

legend avers, I leave for the gentle reader to decide. In old days there was talk of a troll or monster of some kind which ate children and could even swallow a boat, spitting out the nails like cherry stones. It is another colourful reminder that in our remoter areas, semi-pagan beliefs still persist . . .'

The author continued with some philosophical abstractions, and Freddie was on the point of losing interest, when his eye was caught by a paragraph on the opposite page.

'There is a druidical site approximately halfway down the eastern shore which my shepherd guide claimed to be a temple where human sacrifices took place, though it is uncertain where he obtained his information. I pitched my tent at How Rock, and must confess to having spent a night of unusual restlessness and melancholy – which said, I have to report a considerable reluctance to leave – rather as on those cards of invitation which say "The Pleasure of your Company is Requested"!'

The two passages filled Freddie with the first glimmer of excitement he'd felt for days. Of course, he knew these were the 1950s and such things were moonshine, but it did mean there really might be just the ghost of a possibility of a monster in the lake – and as for How Hall, that was where the Seathwaites lived. Their house was probably haunted!

He wanted to tell Bertrand about it, and hurried off down the corridor. The boy was still scribbling.

'Look, Bertrand,' he said, showing him the book, 'it says there was a monster in the lake, at any rate a legend about one. And there were those people in the newspaper who saw one the other day.'

The French boy looked at the opened page, and looked back at his unfinished letter.

'Ah oui,' he said.

Freddie would have liked to bang Ashley Merewether down on his pretty head.

'Come on,' he said, 'let's go out. We can't stay in here all day.'

They put on their raincoats and gumboots – Freddie did not like to call them wellingtons for fear again of offending French sensibilities – collected their packed lunches from the kitchen, and went out into the rain.

Mr Aylott had made it clear in his communications with Freddie's mother that a cooked midday meal was not provided. It was one of the multiplicity of points that had raised Freddie's misgivings.

'You'll be out on the lake or climbing the hills all day,' his mother had assured him. 'Who wants to be cooped up eating stew when all Wordsworth Country lies waiting to be discovered? Wisdom and Spirit of the Universe and so forth. Remember your A Levels next year.'

As they squelched up the drive to join the road that ran up to the lake's end across the river to the hamlet whose cottages and boathouse lay hooded in mist, Freddie brooded upon the work that on first inspection had seemed so utterly dense and dislikeable.

For one thing, there were no rhymes, which made learning it much harder. (Freddie had long ago tumbled to the notion that English exams are best undertaken with a liberal scattering of more or less relevant quotes.) For another thing, the poem seemed to go on and on – rather, as he now perceived, rounding a bend and seeing the limitless expanse of water, like the lake itself.

The French boy sloshed ahead with the hopelessness of the retreat from Moscow but Freddie paused, tasting the rain as it drizzled from his brow, and remembering the words of old 'Gibbers' Thompson as he prescribed Books One and Two for holiday reading.

'Foolish boy,' he had squeaked in that curiously gibbering voice, perhaps the most imitated of all the masters by the school mimics. 'Foolish and newt-hearted boy, do not think that Wordsworth, just because he writes at length in studied and sometimes circumlocutory language – do not fall into the error of supposing that this man was a fusty and passionless blatherer. He was ardent, he was sensitive, he was the arch-Romantic. He fathered a child on a French girl, Annette, and espoused the French Revolution when it was not fashionable to do so. "Bliss was it in that dawn to be alive, but to be young was very heaven." Hm? Though when I look at you, I am comforted at least that youth isn't everything he cracked it up to be. There is an essay there somewhere. Now you go forth. Frolic. But peruse. I do not want anyone next term to be unfamiliar with *The Prelude*.'

Trust Wordsworth to father a child on a mouldy old French girl, thought Freddie, licking nimbus. But wait a minute – wasn't the froggie's name Val something?

'What is your name?' he shouted through the droplets.

'Je m'appelle Bertrand,' muttered the French boy, kicking a stone that jumped like a Jeremy Fisher straight into the water.

'Non, non, non, not Bertrand. Votre autre nom.'

'C'est Vallier.'

Freddie was sure it was the same name as the Annette's. Here was a turn-up for the book. Old Gibbers would go into a five-minute balls scratch when Freddie told him, or even take off his glasses and wind a leg round and round inside his ear for the wax, which he did when he was really worked up.

'Vous êtes descendu de Wordsworth,' Freddie told Bertrand.

'Ah oui,' said Bertrand.

They mooched on in silence. Freddie's momentary

47

elation subsiding like the ripples of a splash. Old Gibbers might scratch for all he was worth or all he was Wordsworth for that matter, but what good would it do him now? He sensed that, in the old canvas fishing knapsack his mother had provided, the packed lunch was already taking in water. It was nearly half past ten. Trickles to left of 'em, trickles to right of 'em, and trickles trickling down the roughened fabric interior of the wellingtons. A group of houses, not more than four or five, hove into view as they sloshed round a corner.

Freddie looked at his waterproof Ingersoll. It was only half past ten. The day stretched before him like Ettenwater and *The Prelude* itself – vast, wet and cheerless. In the distance, he could just hear again the peculiar bass warble that had manifested itself the evening before. Last night it had seemed interesting. Today its mournful honk summed up everything about the place. 'Honk', he recalled, was the school slang for fart. He was momentarily cheered by the irreverent school associations conjured with the word but when he considered the problem of trying to communicate them to Bertrand he became depressed again. He didn't suppose beautiful Bertrand honked.

'Venez,' he said at last, 'regardez la centre ville.'

The French boy gave no indication of response to the joke. He was lost in his private misery, too far away to be reached by the famous English sense of humour.

The centre ville turned out to be a tiny shop, and a pub. The only sign of life came from the shop where a naked bulb inside glowed like a tethered will-o'-the-wisp.

'You would like some chocolate?' suggested Freddie.

He had searched eagerly through the packed lunches – they were the only things that offered any hope of entertainment for the day – but hopes were dashed when inspection through the greaseproof paper seemed to reveal only Spam and cheese sandwiches and an orange. He hated cheese sandwiches, and one could not feel buoyant about Spam unless it was the American sort, which he was sure it wasn't.

Bertrand was stirred into response by the mention of chocolate. He became quite animated.

'Oui, oui,' he said. 'I like well the chocolate.'

Could it be, thought Freddie with a flutter of hope, that his seemingly total lack of English was in fact no more than visitor's initial shock and desperation?

Inside, the shop smelt of paraffin, twine, strawberry icecream, bread and old clothes, but mainly of paraffin. A very little old woman was sitting at the counter, knitting. She did not look up when they entered, even though the bell beat a wild tarantella behind them as Freddie closed the door.

'Good morning,' said Freddie, shyly.

His mother set great store by formal politeness.

'Happen it is,' said the little old lady.

There was a long silence.

Freddie desperately glanced around the crowded little shelves. He was reminded of the Sheep's shop in *Through the Looking-Glass*, and felt convinced that anything he wanted would be similarly unavailable.

There was indeed a profusion of things he didn't need. Oilskins, string, pencils, colouring books, toddlers' clothes, nylon stockings, gumboots, cheap tennis rackets . . . but finally he located a small display of confectionery. Even though they'd lost some of the glamour they'd had when rationed, sweets were still a source of excitement.

'Voilà, Bertrand. Que voulez-vous?'

'Ceci est du chocolat? Mais il n'y a pas de Nestlé.'

Freddie could have shot him.

At the unusual language, the tiny old woman became more animated.

49

'Eh? Foreigners then?'

Freddie debated whether to acquiesce or deny. In the end, it didn't seem to make any difference.

'Sort of,' he said.

'Don't like foreigners,' said the woman. 'Ar't German?'

'No.'

'Don't like Germans. Jackie,' she shouted suddenly, 'Germans.'

'What?' A great voice rumbled from the direction of the oilskins.

Freddie felt it was time to set the record straight.

'We're not Germans. I'm English. My friend is French.'

'Did someone say German?'

A huge bearded man dressed in a grubby fisherman's jersey and corduroys emerged and loomed over them.

'Sprecken sie Deutsch?'

Freddie desperately wanted to go out. The oily raincoat smell, coupled with his goat's milk breakfast, was beginning to make him feel sick. But he suddenly saw, of all things, a copy of *Health and Efficiency* in a little rack devoted to knitting magazines. He knew he had to have it. It was the only thing he had seen around the lake that offered the faintest hope of entertainment.

'I'm sorry,' he said to the giant, 'your mother must have misunderstood. I'm English. My friend is French. N'est-ce pas, Bertrand?'

'Quoi?'

'I'm sorry,' said Freddie, again.

'That's all right, then,' said the big man. 'But if you'd been German, I might have had to take exception. I was in a PoW camp, si'thee. Some scars do not heal. You young people don't remember.'

'I was once when I was small nearly bombed by a doodlebug,' said Freddie. 'We had to shelter under the kitchen table. I remember that. And a fifty-pound bomb dropped in my prep school grounds.'

'Well, that's all right, then. If it hadn't been for the Red Cross food parcels, I'd be pushing up couch-grass in the Stalag cemetery. Mind you, we had a çushy time of it compared with some. On the Burma Railway, like.'

'That's enough of that, Jackie. Doctor said not to dwell on the past,' said the old woman.

'Well. T'Japs were monsters.'

'Jackie,' said the woman, reprovingly.

'Talking of monsters,' said Freddie, changing the subject, 'is it true there's a monster in the lake? Wordsworth saw one when he stole a boat. "A huge shape, dark and huge."'

'Don't know about that,' said the giant. 'I'm about up to t'back teeth wi' Wordsworth too – so would you be if you lived up here.'

Freddie thought the big man was a Wordsworth critic after his own heart. He wished he could put him in a room with Old Gibbers for ten minutes.

'My friend, Bertrand, is related to Wordsworth,' he told the man. 'I'm pretty sure. N'est-ce pas, Bertrand?'

But Bertrand rather surprisingly had discovered the *Health and Efficiency* and was thumbing through it avidly.

'Don't know about that,' said the giant 'He looks more like a proper froggy to me. Look at him goggling at that torso.'

'Jackie,' cautioned the old woman again.

Freddie didn't pursue the matter. There was something else he wanted to know.

'Talking of boats,' he began.

'Steal any boats round here,' said the man, 'and it won't be monsters coming after you, dark and huge.'

'I wasn't thinking of stealing,' said Freddie with dignity.

51

'You can hire a rowing boat for a bob an hour,' replied the giant.

'What about motorboats?'

'No motorboats.'

'But I saw some.'

'No motorboats if you're under eighteen,' said the man. 'It's the insurance. Crippling.'

'All right,' said Freddie. 'We'll have a rowing boat.'

'In this weather?'

'There's nothing else to do.'

'All right,' said the man, who was turning out to be quite a good egg, though you had to watch him. 'I'll untie one for you directly. Anything you want from here meanwhile? Postcards? Mother's got a nice view of the lake. Stamps? Insect repellent? Kendal Mint Cake? Browse by all means.'

'Two Crunchy Bars, please. Oh, and my friend would like that magazine. And we would want the boat sort of now if you don't mind.'

'Suit yourself.'

'That'll be five and six,' said the old woman. 'We don't normally have that book. Somebody ordered it and never collected. It's too natural for folk round here.'

'If I wanted to see a tottie pressed up against a larch tree, I'd go up Hawkshead way and talk t'Land Army lasses,' said the giant.

'Jackie.'

'Sorry, Mother.'

''E never gets to walk out,' said the old woman, 'it's a reet shame.'

'This way, please, gentlemen.'

8

The boys followed Jackie onto a slippery little jetty at the back of the shop. A line of boats, draped in green canvas, shuffled oozily at their moorings.

'First hires we've had all week,' said the giant, not altogether reassuringly. 'It's as wet out of the water as it is in it. Which d'you reckon?'

There was little to choose between the dripping hulks, but Freddie pointed.

'We'll have *Lucy*,' he said. 'That's a poem by Wordsworth. "A slumber did my spirit steal."'

'I know it is and all,' said the giant. 'They're all named after him. 'Twas my idea. I read a lot in the Stalag when I weren't having my head examined. *Lucy*'s popular. There's fewer takers for *Guilt and Sorrow*. You could have *Prelude* if you wanted.'

'*Lucy* will do fine,' said Freddie.

The big man seized the green canvas and tugged it expertly sideways. A small deluge sloshed into the bilgy water.

'Better look sharp,' he said, 'or you'll get wet trousers. And you know what that means. Piles. Which one's going to row?'

'You know how to row?' enquired Freddie, making rowing motions at Bertrand who was standing like a limpet on the quayside, though Freddie noticed that *Health and Efficiency* had disappeared into the folds of his waterproof.

'Ah, si, si, si,' said Bertrand. 'Bien sûr.'

We shall see, see, see, thought Freddie, expecting an

inevitable display of incompetence since the little ruin had shown no particular aptitude for anything so far.

But when the giant put a pair of oars into his hand and pushed them off, the froggy was suddenly galvanized. With expert strokes, he turned the boat around, and they shot off into the drizzle with a satisfying swirl and gurgle.

'Take your time,' shouted Jackie. 'It's a lot of lake. Don't suppose you'll want to swim, but if you do, take care. It's cold, that water. We had a couple of drownings last summer.'

Freddie was by nature a shy and cautious boy. He had a lively imagination which served him up countless poss-ible disasters, and he heard the giant's last-minute advice with considerable misgiving. Mr Aylott had mentioned drowning too. He suddenly realized he might personally have preferred to go for a walk, although there was always the possibility of bulls. What if they capsized in the middle of the lake? It seemed, as the jetty receded and the lake began to widen, that the French boy was intent on taking them there, pulling away ever more lustily as if to taunt Freddie for his fears. The boat seemed pitifully frail in the middle of all that water. What if the wind got up and there were waves – there was twelve miles of lake – and he had seen pictures of lakes in storm? What if there really were a monster?

He peered out anxiously across the surface, observing that the rain had stopped and that, in its place, the mist was once again draping itself listlessly over the surface. Still the French boy struck on, taking them further and further from the shadowy shore. He put his hand in the water. It was indeed icy.

'Eh bien, Bertrand,' said Freddie, trying to sound robust, 'it's a bit boring in the middle of the lake. Voulez-vous faire une reconnaissance of the bank. Of the rivage?'

54

Desperation had made his French almost fluent. The boy looked at him curiously.

'Le rivage est plus intéressant?' he asked.

'Bien sûr,' said Freddie. 'Beaucoup plus intéressant que le milieu de l'eau illimitable.'

'OK,' said Bertrand, with a shrug, and plied the oars again, turning the boat in the direction of the western shoreline opposite Flat Foot.

Bertrand's unexpressed doubts about the potential interest of the bank proved to be well founded. There was a field with some cows in it – not even a bull (which would at least have provided drama from the safety of the water) – there was a little wood with twisted little trees – there was an interval of sloping scrub – and then another field.

Freddie looked at his watch.

It was twelve o'clock.

At least the boat had provided a way of passing the time. An hour hadn't gone so quickly since they'd arrived. But now it began to hang heavily again. Splish, squeak, glup, squeak. He noticed that there was a little more water in the bottom than there had been before. He watched a small spider taking evasive action as the boat rocked. The French boy, as if to counter Freddie's boredom, started to row very fast, close to the shore.

Freddie looked over the side. A great brown stone like an alligator's belly shot by directly underneath him, the boat almost lifting as it passed over it.

'Prenez garde, Bertrand,' he called in alarm, 'there are rocks.'

But it was too late. There was a nasty splintering noise as the bottom struck. It was more of a graze than a crash but it was clearly something better arrested. Freddie almost jumped up in his vexation. Typical frog to go all out for effect, all shout and no shish kebab – as Sergeant-Major Waldron of the School Corps would say.

'You stupid ass,' he shouted, dispensing with politesse and lingo, 'now look what you've done.'

Bertrand's eyes filled with water. Or was it simply the rain which had started again, tipping trickles down the froggy snout?

'Allez,' said Freddie. 'Give me the oars.'

The two boys changed places while the boat rocked perilously, the motion however seeming to free it from the granite slab beneath. They floated silently, revolving in the faint breeze which had come with the rain, while Freddie investigated the damage.

'Voyez l'eau,' said Freddie, gesturing at the water that sloshed at the bottom of the boat, 'tell me if it gets deeper.' He could see no obvious signs of break or crack.

'D'accord,' said the boy, and fixed it with exaggerated concentration, not even gazing at the shore, while Freddie rowed slowly out into deeper water.

As he pulled at the oars Freddie's humour revived. It seemed, after all, that no serious damage had been done. The French boy might have learned a lesson about treating the lake with due respect. And it was quite decent to row, even in the rain, and not to have anyone telling you it was time for lunch.

But thinking of lunch made him feel hungry. Breakfast seemed as far away as Flat Foot, and the long watery morning did finally call for something solid. He glanced at the rucksacks, stowed safely out of reach of the bilge.

'Venez, donc, Bertrand,' he said, pleased with his patois. 'J'ai faim. Est-ce que vous avez faim aussi?'

'Ah oui,' said Bertrand, huddled in the stern, eyes on the water-level.

'Mais nous pouvons pas manger en plein air,' continued Freddie, 'en plein pluie.'

'Ah non.'

A little headland had come into view with what seemed like a deserted boathouse tucked beside it. Freddie rowed gingerly in its direction, keeping a weather eye open for boulders.

9

The doors of the boathouse were open – indeed it was doubtful whether they would ever close again, so rotted were they and so rusty on their hinges – and the roof offered only token resistance to the rain, but it was sheltered and intermittently dry inside.

Without a word, they tied the boat up and clambered out to inspect.

It was empty of everything except an old stove-in pram dinghy which had been dragged onto the jetty and left for dead. Freddie climbed into it with his knapsack and sat down, thinking of his sandwiches. The bench seat immediately snapped and sent him sprawling into the fungusy water which oozed about in what was left of the bottom.

Bertrand burst into laughter.

At any other time, Freddie would have been amazed, even delighted at this manifestation of humour from the boy, but wet-trousered and smelly from the evil juices, and nursing a bruised thigh, he was piqued.

Worse was to come. He discovered that his sandwiches had fallen into the filth, and only one of them was now fit to eat.

He almost cried.

Bertrand continued to laugh. The sound filled Freddie with a blind vindictive fury. It was the frog's fault that his holidays had turned into such a fiasco. And all the nervy little bugger could do was make fun of him.

'You're not wanted here,' he told Bertrand. 'Bugger off back to France. How dare you laugh at me, you nervy little turd.'

Nervy in Freddie's school parlance meant cheeky and it could hardly be expected that an English boy let alone a French one could understand, but Bertrand responded to the word. Instead of bursting into tears (which Freddie had naturally expected), he stopped laughing, and nodded his head.

'Oui,' he said. 'I am nerveux. It is why my mother has sent me to Angleterre. To learn le sang-froid anglais.'

Freddie felt immediately ashamed. Bertrand was going to learn precious little English coolness under fire if he, Freddie, were going to behave like a windy newbug. He suddenly felt better about the boy.

'Ça ne fait rien,' he said, gesturing at his ruined lunch. 'Les sandwiches sont probablement fabriqués du fromage de chèvre.'

But he was wrong. Instead of goat's cheese, Bertrand's only marginally sodden package revealed sandwiches made of a pale crumbly creamy-looking cheese and the Spam, if not American, wasn't the peppery horsemeat served at school. Freddie felt hunger welling up inside him.

They sat down side by side on a groundsheet which Freddie's mother had made him include in his knapsack – a source of bitter complaint at the time – and dangled their feet over the jetty.

Without a word, Bertrand motioned to him to share his sandwiches. They munched stolidly, looking out across the water, momentarily comforted by the act of eating. The lake lay before them implacable, impassive. The rain continued to fall. It was decent of Bertrand to share his food.

When they had finished the sandwiches and the fruit slice and the oranges and the Crunchy Bars they'd bought at the shop, the boys drank their two bottles of lemonade and looked at their watches. It was a quarter to two.

Sheltered in the boathouse, they felt warmer now. There was no question of leaving. It was far too early to think of going back. Besides, there was nowhere else to go.

More in apathy than expectation, Freddie had a last rummage in his haversack and gave a yelp of excitement. Folded in a strip of cotton were four hard little objects which turned out to be miniature liqueur bottles.

Freddie's mother had a rather sporting habit of sending him back to school with a clutch of tiny Grand Marniers, Marie Brizard's Apricot Brandies, Kümmels and Benedictines. The little illicit bursts of exotic warmth were a welcome contrast to the oeufs à la Dunsmere – congealed eggs in a pool of grease – and the other grey and cold staples of public school existence. She had evidently experienced a pang of remorse and put a similar bonne bouche in his knapsack against a rainy day.

'Voilà!' he cried delightedly. 'Cointreau et Cognac. Vous voulez?'

'Ah non,' said Bertrand, 'Maman n'aime pas.'

'Bugger that for a lark,' said Freddie, 'Maman's not going to have it.'

'Ah oui,' said Bertrand. 'You have reason.'

And they both unscrewed the caps of their miniatures and took a small swig. The experience made Bertrand splutter. He had evidently never had strong spirit before, but he reapplied himself to his Grand Marnier and sipped with increasing zeal.

As the warmth permeated the moistness of the afternoon Freddie remembered the *Health and Efficiency* which Bertrand had bought at the shop.

'Allez,' he said, 'perhaps now is the moment for your journal.'

The French boy obediently extracted the publication from his haversack, and they sat side by side, swigging

60

their miniatures and gazing at the Swedish girls' penchant for pressing their buttocks against boulders.

As they sat, side by side, with their bare thighs touching – both wore shorts – gawping at the severely swerving flanks of the Norse goddesses and with the warm tricklings of the brandy imparting a measure of optimism, Freddie's feelings about the holiday at last climbed from the muddy nadir at which they had lurked, flounderlike, since their arrival.

Maybe the whole thing could after all turn out well, especially if they could find more miniature bottles – or maybe at least some beer.

Drinking, even more than smoking, was strictly forbidden at school (even in the holidays anything stronger than cider never appeared on the table, though Rollo was known to have several stiff whiskies before dinner).

Of course, the First Eight were allowed beer with their supper which they took in a special ante-room outside Hall, but that was to build them up. For the rest of College nothing else was countenanced. It made Freddie's mother's little gift all the more quixotic.

As Freddie turned these thoughts over, enjoying the companionable warmth of the brandy and shifting his buttocks, his bare thigh touched Bertrand's and he was suddenly suffused with an almost electric tingle which graduated, he was startled to find, into an erection.

He had reflected only this morning on the disconcertingly erratic nature of the phenomenon. Oh, it had happened often enough; but never sitting quite so close to someone with your winkle actually almost prodding them through the flannel.

He couldn't move. It would seem too suspicious to get up suddenly. Besides the situation was excruciatingly pleasant. The more nervous he became, the more intense grew the pleasure. He knew that if he were going to sit there any longer he would die of embarrassment. What was it the frog had said? Le sang-froid anglais. He'd laugh himself sick if he saw the tell-tale sign in Freddie's trousers.

Freddie stole a quick glance at Bertrand. The boy was sitting there, quite oblivious, turning the pages, making little French whistles and oo la las.

Of course if he'd been a boy at school, Freddie might have told him. They'd have had a quick fumble and that would have been that. Not that Freddie made a practice of that sort of thing. He never really felt like it when it came down to the point. Oh, you could pretend you had a lust for a little man but it was only because they looked like girls.

Perhaps that was it this time. Now he looked at the French boy with his long lashes and angel face, he did seem beautiful; but it wasn't quite that he looked like a girl. There was something at once fresh and despoilable about him, something irresistible and illicit, romantic and carnal; and all the while he sat there, smiling like a faun.

Freddie was desperate. He could feel the beginnings of controllessness upon him . . . when suddenly he was saved by the boy himself.

'Qu'est-ce que c'est que ça? Vite. Regardez, Freddie.'

Freddie dragged his glazed awareness away from the slowly subsiding convolvulus in his trousers and looked out in the direction of Bertrand's outstretched hand.

'Where? What?' he cried. 'Quoi? Qu'est-ce qui arrive?'

A strange disturbance in the water, a raised and eddying swirliness greeted his inspection.

It seemed centred some hundred yards from the shore, and appeared entirely without cause. There was no boat, no wind, even the slight drizzle had momentarily stopped. It was almost as though some great sleek Cumberland sausage was writhing this way and that only inches below

62

the surface. And when the eddy broke from its place and started to swirl towards the boathouse, Freddie felt an impulse to spring to his feet and retreat to the wall behind them, and half did so, and then stopped because it looked so lacking in stiff-upper-lipness.

The French boy appeared to be more intrigued than nervous. They were both disappointed when the eddy subsided into a mere ripple.

'C'est un petit maelstrom,' Bertrand cried. 'A torment of the water.'

'Perhaps it was the monster,' suggested Freddie.

'Monstre? Ah non,' said the French boy scientifically. 'Les monstres n'existent pas.'

'The monsters bally well do exist,' said Freddie. 'You ask the people around Loch Ness. They've taken photographs of it. Some people saw one here too. It was in the papers. Besides there's a legend. So stuff that in your peep and smoke it.'

'What is a ledge end?'

'It is . . . a tradition . . . like mythology . . .'

'Ah . . . légende,' said Bertrand, emphasizing the second syllable. 'C'est vrai qu'on a vu le monstre?'

'C'est très vrai.'

'We could make an observation scientifique, perhaps? No?'

'If you like.'

There was after all nothing else to do. Freddie didn't know quite what the boy meant by scientifique – a log book possibly and other French precisions? But it would serve to pass the time. The French boy was already scrabbling in his pack for a pencil. Freddie remembered that his mother had included a notebook for him to record plants and wildlife. She was keen on such things.

He fished it out and gave it to Bertrand. After all a monster was about as wild as life could get.

While Bertrand consulted his watch and calculated on Freddie's Ordnance Survey map exactly where they were, Freddie was glad of the opportunity to collect his thoughts.

Now that the tide of passion had diminished he felt both ashamed at having been so easily swayed by gross 'inclinasshions', and at the same time frustrated at not having succumbed to them. Then there was this monster business – absurd, of course – Aitken would laugh it out of court. But it opened a doorway, frightening and fascinating, to a world of danger and glory and, yes, romance that he had always sensed – read about, of course but never found.

He wondered what the French boy was thinking. Had he noticed? Why was he smiling in that secret way of his? It was unthinkable to try and confide his feelings. Bertrand would be shocked and tell his mother ,and she would in turn tell his, Freddie's mother, and Rollo would get to hear of it, and the matter would never be forgotten.

No, he would just have to bally well contain himself – take cold showers and go for runs – the Head's prescription for temperance and chastity.

Even so, it did add a dimension to the holiday. He stole another look at Bertrand. Yes, he was definitely more exciting than Peters, and even Lulu seemed a little hoydenish beside him. He wondered whether Wordsworth ever felt horny about Coleridge, Lamb and Southey.

It had stopped raining. Bertrand finished writing in the notebook. The boys looked at each other.

'Allez,' said Bertrand. 'Let me return to where we first saw the monstre.'

He pointed to the spot where the eddy had appeared.

Freddie felt a surge of apprehension. What if there really were a monster? It would rear up, the boat would tip over and they'd vanish without trace in the chilly depths. But he didn't want to seem hopelessly windy, and Bertrand was already making a primitive fishing line with a bent nail, a crumb of Spam, a stone and a length of old twine that was lying at the bottom of their boat.

Collecting the groundsheet and remains of lunch, they put them back in the boat. Freddie had a pee against the wall, while Bertrand, showing the same chasteness with which he dressed, went round the other side of the building.

They embarked.

Freddie rowed while Bertrand cautiously towed his line as the bottom sloped away beneath them.

The lake was still absolutely deserted. The occasional duck scooted about near the shore. A seagull swooped, squawking. The scree on the mountain further up the lakeside whizzed in a frozen forty-five-degree avalanche, straight down like a disaster, to the doors of Grendel's cave.

Keyed up by fear and delight, Freddie swished the skiff across the water, sending a juicy bow-wave shooting out on either side. A line from *The Prelude* crossed his mind. He shouted it aloud:

> 'And as I rose upon the stroke, my boat
> Went heaving through the water like a swan.'

'Comment?' said Bertrand, and then, 'Tiens. Arrêtes. Nous voilà.'

Freddie pushed on his oars and the boat stopped, the lakeside still wheeling about them Wordsworthianly.

The ripples spread, and subsided.

A great silence flattened the water.

They peered down. Nothing disturbed the greenish sultana-coloured depths. Bertrand jiggled his twine.

Freddie opened his mouth to speak but Bertrand lifted a finger in caution.

65

'Le monstre a soixante-dix oreilles,' he said.

Freddie shot him a look. Was he trying to be funny or was this French precision again?

They waited for twenty minutes. It started raining again. The greeny depths turned blind as frosted glass under the insistent droplets. Freddie looked at his watch. It was half past three.

Returning the boat to Jackie and walking back to Flat Foot would take at least three quarters of an hour. There might be a cup of tea there or something. He could read *Health and Efficiency* in the rears (school for double vé cé, Bertrand, comprenez?).

Everyone in sight had warned about the dangers of masturbation, but it did seem to while away the time and besides he was still feeling the effects of that enormous rise.

'Eh bien, Bertrand,' he said.

Just then the boat began to rock. At first it was hardly perceptible, a mere vibration, but it gradually built up to a discernible jostle.

'Ecoute,' said Bertrand.

A sleek line of ripple was whispering towards them from a spot thirty yards away to their right. Freddie was horrified and gripped Bertrand involuntarily. They stared fascinated as the little wave passed under the boat, wriggling the bottom as it went, and raced away towards the shore.

'That was it, Bertrand,' said Freddie, finally. 'That was Him.'

'Monsieur le Monstre,' said Bertrand. 'Je vous salue.'

And he stood up and gave a very creditable military salute for a frog.

Freddie suddenly remembered Wordsworth's girlfriend was called Vallon, not Vallier, so Bertrand wasn't related to him after all. It was a point in his favour.

66

'Asseyez-vous, idiot,' hissed Freddie. 'The boat will bouleverse itself.'

'OK, mon capitaine,' said Bertrand, sitting down beside him on the rower's bench so that his thighs touched Freddie's again, 'but perhaps I row this time?'

Freddie didn't like to argue for fear of being caught again with a monster in his trousers; so Bertrand rowed him in fine style and Freddie sat in the stern and pulled up his hood and watched the raindrops skedaddling down his nose.

They were within three hundred yards or so of the quay when he suddenly realized there was a great deal of water in the boat.

'Vite, Bertrand,' he shouted, 'we're bloody well sinking.'

Bertrand rowed with a will but the faster he went, the more the water rushed in. They arrived at the jetty just in time to clamber out and watch their craft settle into the ooze.

Jackie appeared looking grave.

'What have yer done, young 'un?' he enquired. 'Knocked it agin a rock, 'ave yer?'

His accent was thicker than this morning. He smelt slightly of beer.

'It was all right, honestly,' protested Freddie. 'We did have a little scrape but it was all right until just now.'

'You might ha' drowned yourse'n. Where would yer be then?'

'Under the whelming tide, visiting the bottom of the monstrous world,' said Freddie.

Lycidas was another of his set books. He was glad to be on dry land with a quote to hang his hat on.

'All right, clever clogs. But I wouldn't like to be in your shoes when Mother sees you.'

67

'Oh come on, Jackie. It was an accident. We won't do it again. How much do we owe?'

Jackie leant over, grasped the waterlogged vessel in both hands, tipped it over to let the water drain out and swung it up as if it were a toy. He inspected the bottom briefly, sucking his teeth. There was an area near the bows where splinters showed palely amongst the paint.

Freddie's heart sank. His mother had given him enough money to amuse themselves but not to pay for heavy repairs – besides there was always the possibility that they would be banned from the boatyard – and what on earth would they do then?

At last Jackie delivered his verdict.

'That'll be five shilling for the time. Gi' us another five bob and we'll call it a day.'

Freddie almost cried with relief. Ten shillings was just affordable.

'Did you ever see anything in the lake?' Freddie asked as the giant took them to the shed where he kept the boat money.

'Here? In t'lake?'

'Yes, Jackie.'

'Oh, I seen things right enough.'

'What sort of things?'

'Contraceptives I seen. After Bank Holiday.'

'Monsters?'

'Big ones, yes.'

'Not contraceptives, Jackie. I mean monsters. Something that lives in the lake. It's very deep, isn't it?'

Jackie paused, his great head swooping about like a tethered condor.

'We don't talk of monsters,' he said at last. 'Frighten the tourists. Or encourage 'em. Can't recall which. It's bottomless, you know.'

And that was all Freddie could get out of him. The boys trudged back in silence – the rain, now blowing straight up their backs, discouraged the head-swivelling necessary for conversation.

10

Upon reaching Flat Foot, they found Mrs Aylott and Isobel in the hall putting up antlers.

'I have been beside myself with lust all day,' said Isobel in French. 'My body is one continual torment of flame. My blood is on fire. Come to me quickly, oh charming stranger, lest I die.'

'There's one subject she's going to have no trouble with in her exams,' said Mrs Aylott fondly. 'Viva voce French. If only she'd apply herself, she'd be Grammar School material.'

'Pourquoi ne bouillez-vous pas la tête?' enquired Freddie, acidly.

'Ta gueule,' said Bertrand.

'Yes, she is a nice girl,' said Mrs Aylott. 'Underneath.'

Isobel stuck her tongue out at both of them when her aunt's back was turned but a shout from the kitchen brought the conversation to a halt.

'Go and see what your uncle wants, dear, while I finish this last head. There's tripe tomorrow. It has to stew two days. He has a wonderful way with tripe. Tripe in goat's milk.'

Freddie cancelled his desire for tea. He had forgotten about the goat's milk. And it would no doubt be brought by the obnoxious slutlet along with further douceurs for Bertrand.

A flicker of suspicion crossed his mind that he might just possibly be jealous, but the notion was absurd. When they had washed and changed, Freddie suggested to Bertrand that he read the paper with the bit about the monsters in it, in the Res Lounge, and sent him off with his dictionary.

He then extracted the *Health and Efficiency* from Bertrand's haversack, and went into the lavatory.

11

Freddie himself had discovered an unquestionable talent for masturbation in his second term, shortly after his fourteenth birthday.

He had known, of course, that his tool went stiff. It would ache in a pleasant sort of way. But nothing would happen.

His preparatory school headmaster had explained, in a half-hour's embarrassing leavers' sex-talk, the theory and practice of the sexual act, but nobody at the school – apart from Barthop – a giant of a lad who was rumoured to be having an affair with the under-matron Rowena, and Henshaw, who was certainly having an affair with the school butler – had the definitive word on what it actually felt like.

Somehow no one liked to ask Barthop or Henshaw – the one because he was so big and the other because there was an instinctive feeling that what he was doing was 'not done'.

A clown called McGregor who would do anything for a laugh would sometimes lie on his bed during Sunday morning late lie-in and wiggle his silly little pencil. And that was about it.

However, with Freddie's arrival at public school, there had been a leap into worldly wisdom.

For the first year, the boys shared a Junior Common Room in their House. The majority consisted of boys who had just arrived at the beginning of the school year. But there were several others with one or two terms' seniority, and these of course ruled the roost, impressing the newbugs with their knowledge of the ropes.

If this minority were of unruly or malevolent temperament, they would make the others' lives hell – as well as instructing them in smut.

Newbugs quickly learned how many of their jacket buttons they should keep done up, and what was the nickname of the Housemaster of B House.

There was a formal written test on such topics which was acknowledged and indeed fostered by the school, but there was also an unwritten interrogation by the Junior Common Room seniors at the end of the first term on things like knowing all three verses of 'The Foggy Foggy Dew' (which was considered the very acme of innuendo), and being able to sing 'The Good Ship Venus'.

If you failed, you were given a 'lacing', which meant you had to run round the ping-pong table while being hit by all the rest of the Common Room with cricket bats, hockey sticks or anything they could lay their hands on. Everyone got a lacing sooner or later but it was definitely a thing to be avoided.

Freddie, a hitherto rather modest child, had discovered an aptitude for learning verse. He soon acquired a ripe litany of limericks culled from his elder brother's own extensive repertoire.

'Know-All' Newall, the ringleader of the seniors, never tired of listening to 'The Bey of Algiers' and 'The Young Girl of Darjeeling'.

'God,' he used to say admiringly, 'you've got a filthy mind, Pemberton.'

All Freddie really wanted to do was to avoid being laced.

Newall was soon expelled for overstepping the school's considerable tolerance. One of the pretty juniors whom he had chased round the ping-pong table once too often complained to his merchant banker father. There had been a shake-up. Intimidation was put in abeyance. The Chaplain interviewed all concerned, put his hand on your knee, urged you to tell him more and to let him know if anyone tried to get inside your trousers in a form-room cupboard. His door was always open.

Through all this, though much discussed, the mystery of the orgasm remained.

The matter was finally settled some eighteen months back when Freddie was fourteen and a half.

One night in the Michaelmas Term, having primed himself exhaustively on the theory, and suitably inflamed by the picture of an impossibly leggy lovely on an empty box of stockings which Surtees's mother had sent a cake in, Freddie had settled himself down for a rub.

The problem, he had found, was what to keep your mind on when you were doing it.

He had torn off the top of the box, and had secreted the leggy lovely between the sheets – but he had to keep switching on the torch under the bedclothes to remind himself of what she looked like. Her wild, wild eyes, full of vacuous roguishness, gazed back on his furtive applications, her exquisitely hosed shanks with their welted stocking-tops arched and taut, a fitting siren to lure semen onto the shoals.

Then there was the problem of not letting Braybrook know what he was up to.

Braybrook was notorious for exposing wankers. He was always calling out about Biddulph on the other side. Biddulph just guffawed but Freddie knew that he, Freddie, would be mortified.

Silence, then, was of the essence.

He found that if he very gently agitated his tool against the sheet, the resultant friction produced a certain not unpleasant itchy sort of response.

It was around this point in his rubbing that he generally fell asleep. But this time he gritted his teeth, pinched himself to keep awake, and rubbed on.

Around him, the sounds of raillery and chunks of Norwegian caramelized goat's cheese (brought back by Ole Boetke, whose father believed in English education and Norwegian cheese) subsided.

Freddie rubbed on. He could hear even the prefects on their way to bed now, larking about in the bathroom with the milk.

He grew desperate. Was he going to have to rub all night? Was he some kind of freak? His tool was growing quite sore at the end, and there was still no sign of conclusion.

At last, slowly, he became aware of something stirring in the depths. Concentric circles of pleasurable discomfort echoed around his loins. He wanted to stop but he couldn't. He began to panic. Something terrible was happening. He was about to undergo some kind of seizure. He had done it wrong. He was going to explode, blood fountaining from his shattered stem, split like a bulrush.

The leggy lovely fell to the floor, followed with a clatter by the torch.

A great siphoning of something shot out of him onto the sheet.

Ooof.

He lay exhausted, satiety mingling with terror. Cautiously he felt about and discovered reservoirs of stickiness. There seemed so much. It must be blood. In his fright, he was also conscious of the embarrassment of having to go and tell the matron. He decided he would rather die.

A voice from the other side of the cubicle wall called out:

75

'I say, chaps, Freddie is tossing.'

The whole episode still brought him out in a cold sweat when he thought about it.

One of the other things that Freddie learned, next day, was in future to try and conceal and indeed avoid any tell-tale little discoloured starchy patches on the sheet, for it was just the sort of evidence that Braybrook pounced on. (Naturally he never had any on his own scrawny linen.) From the start, the essential elements in masturbation were guilt and concealment.

So now, eighteen months later and many a wank wiser, Freddie settled himself on the vitreous enamel Derwentwater of the guesthouse, and turned the pages of *Health and Efficiency* with practised hand, searching for the most lust-inspiring photograph.

He settled finally on a picture of a young lady crouched like a Queen's Beast on a great slab of glacial rock. Her breasts were the nearest thing to invitation in the magazine, and there was just a snatch of a glimpse of pubic hair, a luxury which the editor normally tried to avoid.

This was the one. Freddie closed his eyes and tried to imagine what it would be like to clutch at those bosoms, fondle that foliage, plunge precipitately between those shanks. His hand was already straying to his person when he had the sudden instinct that he was not alone.

It seemed ridiculous. This lav wasn't like the school rears with a gap a foot high under the door, and bore holes through the knots in the wood, so you might as well have a crap in the Clock Quad for all the privacy you got. No, this was a proper bog.

However, swivelling round in precaution, he noted that a small frosted window behind was unlatched, and that a head with a pair of beady little eyes was bobbing up and down outside trying to look in – and, it seemed, intermittently succeeding.

It was Isobel, the shit.

Freddie was torn between rage and agitation. How dare the little harpy try to muscle in on his private performance! He might've been having a very serious crap.

At the same time, he had to admit, he hadn't been. What if she told her aunt and uncle that they had a shameful self-abuser under their roof? The thing didn't bear contemplation. It would all lead straight back to Rollo again.

How much, if anything, had she seen?

After due reflection, he decided that a crap would be the best form of defence. Even in his extremis, he relished the phrase. Aitken would pee himself. But this was no time for scatological self-indulgence – or any other kind for that matter. He would pretend he hadn't seen her, and was merely looking round to check the lav paper.

A genuine crap, of course, was out of the question. Even if he had wanted to, he couldn't do it when he knew he was being watched. So, instead, he made a few heaving, grunting noises, and finally threw a pellet of chewing gum into the pan to make a convincing plop. It didn't. It made a pathetically weedy little splish and rolled about forlornly at the bottom looking as if it would never flush out, in which case the finger was sure to be pointed at him by the saturnine Aylott. Anxious to avoid trouble, he pushed a large wodge of paper on top of it and pulled the plug.

It didn't work. The chain rattled and clanked, but never a drop of water did it unleash.

Freddie was growing flustered. He pulled it again urgently. It bounced and bucked, dislodging a few speckles of rust, but nothing more significant happened. He gave it a vicious tug, picturing Bertrand and the Aylotts to say nothing of Isobel the Obnoxious lined up outside, aghast at the mayhem he was wreaking on the Derwentwater.

He tried every conceivable kind of pull from the coaxing to the overtly vindictive. He crept up on it and took it by surprise. He said a prayer. He tried a spell which Aitken said was infallible. Finally, just as he was about to give up, resigning himself to a red-faced emergence – how would he explain the volumes of paper with only a pod of chewing gum to justify it? – it suddenly operated. The water deluged down. He almost cried with relief.

However, when the swirl subsided, he was greeted by the spectacle of several yards of soggy tissue rolled into an impenetrable ball and completely blocking the bowl with no doubt the errant chewing gum still snugly tucked underneath it.

There was nothing for it but to plunge his hand into the vitreous recesses and take the whole thing out.

He squeezed the excess of water from the mess as best he could, wrapped the soggy residue into a ball, tucked it underneath his jacket, and cautiously opened the door.

The corridor was miraculously empty. Doubtless Bertrand was still in the Res Lounge. Freddie decided to hide the awful lumpen sogginess in his wardrobe for the moment, and think of somewhere to put it later. He needed time to consider. Secreting it under his jacket he shot along the passage and threw open the door of their room.

Bertrand was sitting on his bed looking glumly out of the window.

This was something for which Freddie was totally unprepared. How could he explain to Bertrand just exactly why he was rushing around Flat Foot with yards of wet lavatory paper in his hands? The predicament was too ludicrous. Bertrand – for whom he now nursed the most extraordinary assortment of feelings – would give one of those stale-fish froggy looks down his nose.

Gargling an indistinguishable explanation, he rushed back into the corridor just in time to see Isobel emerging from the lavatory with his copy of *Health and Efficiency*, and walking back smartly towards the hall.

Capering with embarrassment and fear, and still clutching his armful of wet bog roll, he darted into the Res Lounge and out through the French windows onto the lawn. Ahead of him were the outbuildings and the tethered goats. His fevered brain grabbed at a solution. For the first time, he was glad to see the goats. Were they not renowned for their omnivorousness?

There was no one to be seen. The Aylotts were doubtless still in the kitchen. The child Isobel would be goggling at the magazine somewhere, deciding what she was going to do about embarrassing him.

Freddie advanced on the goats. They cropped the grass contentedly.

'Here you are,' he crooned. 'Good goats. Have some nice lavvy paper.'

He cast it down before them, tearing it into little clumps, trying to make it look toothsome. They stared at him quizzically.

'Go on, blast you,' he said.

He picked up a morsel and thrust it into the nanny's mouth. He watched her rolling it about her chops like a dowager sampling Sevruga. Finally – he could have kissed her – she started to tuck in. The billy, encouraged by her assent, began to browse among the Bronco on his own account.

'Bon appétit,' Freddie adjured them, and hurried back towards the house.

The mountains frowned at him across the water.

12

Isobel served them their high tea; a Cumberland sausage, no less, coiled like a sea-serpent, its tail dangling over the side of their plate.

Bertrand wrinkled his nose in alarm.

'What is zis?' he demanded.

'C'est un pénis d'éléphant,' she replied demurely.

'Look here,' protested Freddie, but not too strongly because he didn't know quite how she was going to react to the events of the afternoon.

'You look here,' retorted Isobel, drawing the copy of *Health and Efficiency* out of her jumper. 'That's where you were looking. I'll tell my auntie if you give me any trouble. Jerking off in the lav for all to see.'

'I wasn't jerking . . . I . . .'

'Je faisais une drôlerie,' she said to Bertrand. 'C'est une espèce de saucisson de la région, comme saucisse de Toulouse.'

'I do not like saucisse,' said Bertrand.

'Eh bien. Donne-moi ton saucisson,' she winked fulsomely, 'et je te donnerai quelque chose de plus savoureuse.'

'Oh shut up,' said Freddie, recklessly, rushing to protect Bertrand who had started to blush.

'I'm going to tell my auntie of you,' said Isobel, flouncing out.

That's done it, thought Freddie.

'What is ze matter wiz zat girl?' asked Bertrand. 'Why 'as she my periodical in her pull?'

Freddie shrugged, bracing himself for Mrs Aylott's wigging; but it wasn't Auntie who came in, but Mr Aylott with a face like thunder.

'One of you lads been giving toilet paper to my goats?'

13

Freddie's sleep was fitful that night. Whether because of the sausage, the monster or his unruly passions, he would have found it difficult to apportion. Indeed, in his dreams they seemed at times to fuse into one extensive elongation which Mr Aylott insisted on chopping up and feeding to Billy and Nanny.

He woke unrefreshed and looked across to where Bertrand slept, self-contained and composed, wondering what he would do if he slipped into bed beside him and gave him a French polish, and hastily dismissing the thought as ignoble.

They never did that sort of thing in *The Lion, the Witch and the Wardrobe* or indeed in *The Big Six* or *Swallows and Amazons* – approved reading that he had only recently put aside.

Besides, Bertrand would doubtless squeal like the undead, and demand to go home, and Rollo would never let him forget it.

Freddie lay nursing his frustration, and catching the drips in his handkerchief, while the rain tricked down outside contributing its own myriad dribblings to the occasion.

He felt at once better and worse. The immediate itch was relieved, but had he irremediably weakened himself for the day ahead?

'Billiards' Gwilliam, the Senior Cricket Master, whose other great subject was beating, said tossing off interfered with your eye and you should never do it before a match, although he had personally interviewed Freddie, on the eve of umpiring the big fixture with Sherborne, about his recent caning by the Head of School for being late for Chapel, and Billiards had got the most enormous erection while Freddie enumerated the strokes – so what was sauce for the goose clearly wasn't sauce for the Gwilliam.

The Chaplain had it on good authority that Satan, after every emission, could be admitted through the penis.

Dr Pliny-Grace, the psychologist employed by the school to see the juniors through puberty, said its effects were cumulative though non-specific, but a lacklustre academic and sporting career could be confidently anticipated. Whereas Old Squarey the Classics Master, who knew a thing or two and could quote 'Do you remember an inn, Miranda?' with the most luxuriant gestures, completely forgetting the lesson of the day if you got him in the right mood, said the trouble with masturbation was that it could get out of hand.

The accepted wisdom among the boys was that it could give you shag-spots, and if you wanked more than once a day, you could have fits and go mad.

From all this wealth of advice, Freddie tended to follow the boys' prescription, and rationed himself sedulously; but he was always on the look-out for signs of derangement. He lay now monitoring his hands for the shakes and, finding no tremor, started to recite 'There's a breathless hush in the close tonight' to test his frontal lobes.

Raising his eyes when he got to 'His captain's hand on his shoulder smote', he saw that Bertrand was awake and looking at him.

'Bonjour, Bertrand,' he mumbled sheepishly, hoping the French boy hadn't noticed the stirring under the bedclothes.

'Bonjour à toi, Freddie.'

It gave Freddie an unexpected quirk of satisfaction to be called 'toi'.

'We seek the monster today, no?'

Bertrand's English was coming on by leaps and bounds. Good froggy. Freddie considered his suggestion. There was a distinct lack of alternatives to monsters, fabulous or otherwise.

'We seek the monster,' he agreed. 'But we do not tell anyone. It is our secret until we have proof.'

He enjoyed the feeling of confederacy.

The child Isobel did not show up with the tea this morning. Perhaps it had been a first-day privilege yesterday, or maybe she was simply in a bate today; it didn't matter. If Bertrand was prepared to be amenable and speak English, things were definitely looking up.

They dressed and wandered over to the dining room. Here there was a bonus. Deliciously bland if blue-looking cow's milk was on the table. It turned the cornflakes into an orgy.

At length Isobel appeared with a trayful of bacon.

'See what you done,' she said contemptuously to Freddie. 'You loused this one up real good.'

'I beg your pardon?'

'The goats are all blown up with gas. My uncle's going to kill you.'

Freddie chewed thoughtfully on a piece of bacon bone.

'I'm sorry to hear that.'

'What ya want to give 'em shit-paper for anyway? Dumbo.'

'I would like to remind you, Isobel, that I am a guest in this establishment.'

'Not for much longer, you ain't.'

'I told your uncle that I'm very fond of goats. I wanted to give them a special treat. Everyone knows that goats love paper.'

'Go fug yourself. Ton ami,' she addressed herself exclusively to Bertrand, 'ton ami est foutu. Il est frotteur.'

'Go and boil your head,' said Bertrand.

Freddie clapped his hands with glee at the unexpected vernacular. Isobel was so miffed, she walked straight out of the room, biting her lip.

The boys addressed themselves to tea and toast. A gust of wind rattled the window, driving long slicks of rain diagonally across it. Even monster-hunting seemed to be ruled out.

Isobel re-entered in silence and plonked their packed lunches down in front of Bertrand – two crinkly little greaseproof reproaches.

'Womens,' said Bertrand to Freddie as she walked out.

'Ta soeur,' she opened the door and called back.

Bertrand gave Freddie a Gallic shrug. They finished their breakfast in silence, the two packed lunches sitting ominously before them, implacable reminders that at some stage they must set out. Freddie remembered the French verb, 'saillir'. Nobody could possibly be expected to saillir in such a downpour.

They got up, walked into the hall, opened the front door, hurriedly shut it again, mooched in the Res Lounge, returned to their room. Bertrand started a letter. Freddie had a prolonged crap – a genuine exercise this time, in the lavatory next to the dining room, with a good working Derwentwater in it with a much more fluent pull.

Finally the inactivity palled. They put on their coats and wellingtons and went out.

'Saillir is the same as the English word sally,' explained Freddie to Bertrand, quoting 'Twitcher' Ricketts.

Bertrand opened his mouth and shut it again.

The wind was driving the clouds low over the lake, and the mountain tops had disappeared. The wind seemed about Force 20, what Freddie's old Nanny used to call Tom Piper weather, 'The wind will blow my topknot off.'

Their steps seemed to take them automatically on yesterday's road. It wasn't the weather for originality even though the prospect of boating subsided the nearer they drew to the water. It did not look prepossessing. Instead of the pitter-pattery calm of yesterday, the surface was chafed by menacing waves which frothed against the shingly shale in a welter of flotsam.

They walked faster than they had done yesterday although the wind did its best to stop them, blowing their coats into grotesque Michelin Man rotundities.

Freddie anticipated their rejection on arrival, indeed was hoping for it – the water did really look quite evil – and sure enough Jackie was standing in his hut, wagging his head over-emphatically.

'No boats today,' he intoned. 'There's more wind forecast. You'd be swamped before you got to Shadd Point, and then you'd be eels' meat.'

Freddie's relief was tempered by the thought of the day stretching away before them with nothing to fill the boating's place.

'But what are we going to do?' he asked, hopelessly.

'Know what I'm going to do,' said Jackie. 'I'm going to mend the boat you buggered up yesterday.'

'Do you need any help?'

Freddie hated carpentry. It was a measure of his desperation.

'Can't abide people gawping over me. Makes me hit my thumbs.'

There wasn't even another copy of *Health and Efficiency* in the shop. Freddie had told Bertrand about the incident in the lavatory, intimating that he had gone in to have a read, had been driven out by Isobel's prurient peeping, and that in his confusion she had snitched the magazine. Bertrand had looked duly shocked.

86

'She is teeth,' he had commented.

'Thief,' corrected Freddie.

'She is teef, but alors, she is a little derange-ed . . .'

'Cuckoo,' said Freddie.

'Coucou girl.'

The idea of going back to Flat Foot and swotting up on Wordsworth was unendurable even on such a day as this. There was only one thing left to do if they didn't want to lurk in the paraffiny shop all morning goggling at curled-up postcards of the peaks.

'Venez, I mean viens, or do I mean viennes donc,' Freddie said, finding the second person singular had conjugative drawbacks to its intimacy, 'what I really mean is, we'd better go and visiter Mr and Mrs Seathwaite.'

'Seeswaite?'

'She is the daughter, the fille, d'un cousin par mariage de ma grand-mère.'

The connection did seem tenuous even as Freddie described it. Bertrand could not be expected to understand Freddie's mother's enthusiasm for anything she regarded as 'social', and that you could never go anywhere without Mother knowing someone nearby who was a friend of a cousin or indeed a cousin of a friend.

So it was with Mrs Seathwaite. It was doubtful whether Freddie's mother had even met her, but she was a connection, and the daughter of an Honourable to boot, and that was good enough.

A letter had accordingly been despatched to How Hall asking La Seathwaite whether she would keep an eye on the boys, which really, in Freddie's mother's parlance, meant having them round to tea.

'Perhaps she has a tennis court,' his mother had said brightly, knowing Freddie's fondness for the game.

'You can't play tennis by yourself,' Freddie had replied,

turning her earlier argument against her. 'I bet the Frog Prince doesn't play. I bet he can only play French Cricket.'

'I think he's learning,' Freddie's mother said vaguely. 'Anyway, don't be so negative, darling.'

At all events, Mrs Seathwaite had replied – not effusively, it was true – but she had intimated in an ambiguous sort of way that of course the boys could come round any time, she would be only too happy.

It wasn't much to go on, back at home, but it was even less up here, in the rain, with water shooting down the tip of your nose as if it was the Cresta Run, but at this point Freddie was prepared to try anything. It was at least a mile and a half's walk – Mother had shown him exactly where the house was on the map – and it could even be a wasted journey, for there was no guarantee that a single Seathwaite would be in.

But it was better than the only other thing, Wordsworth apart, that Freddie could think of doing, and that was mucking out the sick goats. Well, it wasn't quite the only other thing he could think of doing, but that would have involved a copy of *Health and Efficiency*, or a very wrinkly old photograph from *Esquire* which he kept for emergencies in a recess at the side of his suitcase, and anyway, he'd had his statutory one today already. He didn't want to go into involuntary spasm.

It was a long walk in the icy rain, and both boys had rivulets oozing down their necks and wellingtons by the time they arrived at the driveway to How Hall.

They knew it was How Hall because it said so in black letters on the white gates – gates that were firmly shut.

Freddie had a fear of large dogs.

At places like this, it was a virtual certainty that there

would be a baying Alsatian lying in wait somewhere, ready to come springing out of the rhododendrons, dead keen to bury its fangs in your vitals.

What did one do to dissuade a savage dog? Stand there with a stiff upper lip while it gnawed you to the bone? Strike it and enrage it further? It was the kind of information Rollo was singularly useless at passing on. Freddie always meant to have a pocketful of aniseed balls for just such a contingency, but somehow they were never to hand.

What Bertrand was thinking was as usual impossible to guess.

His beautiful face, with water glistening upon the ferny fronds of his eyelashes, wore a buttoned-up expression in wich no emotion was traceable.

Freddie turned back to the drive. It wound upward beyond the gate between thick shrubbery, and after thirty or forty yards, completely disappeared from view. It went on like that for a quarter of a mile according to the map. The rhododendrons dribbled as only rhododendrons can. Little rivulets scuttled down the drive joining up near the gate into a miniature torrent which disappeared beneath the road. Freddie crossed the tarmac to see whether it reappeared. It did.

His attention now turned to a smaller gate this side of the highway which said 'How Boathouse. Private. Trespassers will be Pros' in faded lettering. An overgrown track beyond it dribbled down towards the lake.

A decision had to be taken. Bertrand was waiting patiently as an ox.

Freddie was seized with an overpowering urge not to go any further, to return to the discomforts of Flat Foot and read Wordsworth, anything rather than stand here in this melancholy menacing place with its potential dogs and its prisoning rhododendrons and its Trespassers will be Pros, to say nothing of its human sacrifices.

There was definitely a custodial air about the place.

> 'Shades of the prison house begin to close
> About the growing boy . . .'

He shook himself, sending a little whirligig of water scattering across the tarmac. It was impossible to go back. He could hardly tell Bertrand, having lugged him here through the downpour, that he was too windy to go any further. Dog or no dog, they must do what they had set out to encompass. It was what his Housemaster had always said. Nothing worthwhile is achieved without effort.

He opened the gate to the drive, and without a word they began to trudge up towards the house. In his anxiety about dogs he tried to walk delicately like Agag, but Bertrand resolutely clanked along, seeming to go out of his way to drag his boots on the gravel.

No hounds appeared, however, and in due course the curving rhododendrons afforded a view of a large granite-built house with faded white windows surrounded by an overgrown lawn and surprisingly immaculate flower-beds.

There was no sign of life – no smoke from the chimneys, no half-open windows. The place seemed to Freddie to have that dead look he had noticed once when his mother had taken him, for some obscure beekeeping reason, to a seaside resort in winter.

Still, no dog slavered beneath the classical porch, and Freddie, gathering courage, walked up to the front door and boldly rang the bell.

It was one of those disconcerting instruments that give you no indication of whether they are actually working. Freddie, on his various excursions round the village for his mother – selling raffle tickets, delivering Christmas presents to cleaning-women, returning change for Women's Institute subscriptions – was familiar with the syndrome, but it didn't help now. His first push yielded no palpable jangle, the second no distant trill, hum or buzz.

The predictable embarrassed waiting period followed. He walked out from under the porch and looked up at the house. He just half felt, as he emerged from the portico, that he'd seen out of the corner of his eye a movement somewhere in a window above him. He turned and gazed at the window intently. The flicker was not repeated.

Bertrand waited, more like a dobbin now, in the rain; stupidly patient, devoid of will.

Freddie went through the familiar self-debate. Would it be rude to ring again? He decided it would; waited some more; wondered whether he had pressed the bell firmly enough; returned to the door and gave it a great squidgy application from every angle. Still no reply.

Freddie noticed that Bertrand had moved slightly, and was now standing under a little spurt of water that came from a leaky gutter over the porch. It seemed to have no impact on him whatsoever. He had lost the ability to register.

Freddie applied the heavy knocker, abandoning the bell. He could hear the sound reverberating inside the hall, running up the staircase, chasing the shadows down the corridors. No one inside could possibly be in any doubt that somebody was wishing to pay a call.

The echoes subsided. Silence resumed.

He was reminded suddenly of a game his mother had played with him when he was a little boy. She had made a little aperture with her knuckles so that, if approached from the side, it made a tunnel.

'Knock, knock,' he had to say, 'anybody at home?'

91

'Yes,' she would reply in a gruff voice, 'it's Mr Fox. Do come in.'

'Oh, thank you.'

Here he would insert his forefinger into the aperture.

'It's young Master Chicken, isn't it?' she would ask.

'That's right.'

'What are you doing in this neck of the woods?'

'I was out for a walk and got lost.'

'Dear me. You must be tired. Well, sit you down. I was just going to have some breakfast. Care to join me?'

'Oh, thank you. What are you going to have for breakfast?'

'Well, I rather think it's going to be chicken.'

The object of the game was to extract your finger with all speed after you had said the obligatory 'good morning', before Mother could close her fingers and trap you. She was very good at the game. It used to give Freddie the most delicious comfortable terror, evoking squeals of joy and fear.

It seemed to him suddenly that this big grey house might contain another and very different Mr Fox, and though he was a long way from a little boy he was still only on the threshold of grownupness. A childlike fear swept over him. He didn't want the door to open now.

'Good morning,' he said to the house.

Without looking at Bertrand, he turned and trudged back down the drive. After all, they could still try the boathouse.

14

Aitken would have enjoyed the TRESPASSERS WILL BE PROS joke, thought Freddie, but there seemed little point in explaining the prostitute jest to Bertrand; besides, he himself wasn't feeling exactly like a good snigger at the moment.

His mother would blithely barge through any gate, enter any field (even if it were full of militant bullocks), walk up any front garden; and Freddie had accompanied her on many such enterprises, dying a thousand deaths when red-faced men appeared shouting – though to her credit it had to be said that she always seemed to be able to pacify them with talk of stinking hellebore or spotted sandpiper noted on their property.

Now, however, there was no mother, only the beautiful French boy with whom he felt half in love as with easeful death. In fact, easeful death seemed infinitely preferable to a red-faced roaring man at the bottom of a slithery track, quite possibly armed with a shotgun, who would give you a very dis-easeful death. What had bloody Wordsworth done when he roamed around as a lad? You never heard of him being charged by bullocks or being warned off for mooning at daffodils on other people's land.

However, there was nothing for it. The thing had to be done. He pushed open the gate and set off down the path, with Bertrand falling in sluggishly behind him.

They had not gone more than thirty yards when, round a bend, another faded sign appeared which made Freddie's knees turn to junket.

'BEWARE THE D–,' it said, and just in case you had a French boy in tow, again 'CHIEN MECHANT'.

They had clearly arrived at the property whose side entrace they had found on their first day.

The French words seemed to galvanize Bertrand out of his torpor.

'Notty dog,' he said.

'I know,' said Freddie. 'I know it's a bally notty dog. No need to rub it in.'

Now more than ever, Freddie wanted to turn back, but Bertrand was contemplating the peeling sign intently.

'If it is notty,' he pronounced, 'it is very old.'

That was it, then. Bertrand had effectively cancelled any chance of retreat. Freddie could almost feel the canines splishing round his throat as in Maupassant's 'The Vendetta' (undertaken last term with Twitcher).

Down they went, through another of those wretched dripping tunnels of rhododendrons, emerging onto a grassy bank where a granite boathouse lay fringed by trees on a little inlet of the lake. It was a stout building, slate roofed, solidly built against the lakeland winters, and doubtless snug inside.

Out here where they stood exposed, out of the cover of the hill and the sheltering dendrons, it was a very different matter. The rain crashed down almost horizontally, driven by the west wind, while, beyond, the lake surface wagged in an endless procession of sprayfringed rollers.

The boys advanced into the lee of the building where there was a small window set in the stone. Cautiously, Freddie crouched and peeped in.

The scene revealed to his gaze was cosy if confused. There was a sagging old leather-covered armchair, and a table with two rickety dining-room chairs drawn up to it, and another smaller gate-legged table, and a desk with a curly-armed chair at its side. All of these were covered with books, dirty crockery, clothes, glasses, whisky bottles (Freddie recognized some of Rollo's favourite brands), writing paper, a megaphone, a string of bunting and a butterfly collection.

Then there was another table, this time in pine, with an array of apothecary-like shelves behind it, all filled with what appeared to be wireless and even television equipment. (Television was new, but some of the richer families around had got it, and at school they'd taken one to pieces in the Science Lab with 'Stinks' Fitton, so he knew a cathode ray tube when he saw one.)

There was an iron army stove with an angular iron pipe doing a half zigzag on its way up to the roof.

There was a tabby cat lying on a pile of old clothes in front of the stove which, judging from the tattered wisp flitting from the chimney, was barely alight. There was a huddle of fishing rods.

There was no sign of a shotgun. Or of a dog.

In the corner of the room, so that Freddie had to crane neck-crickingly round to see it, there was somebody asleep on a truckle bed.

The general effect of the room, though untidier than any boating person he had ever met would countenance, had at the same time the impression of being wonderfully snug – especially to one peeping outside stranded in a dress rehearsal for the Second Flood.

Cheered by the absence of hound or shooter, and with his boyish sense of rectitude affronted by the notion of someone sleeping until after noon, he moved less cautiously up to the next window, motioning to Bertrand to join him. (Bertrand had gone into a state of addle again and was mooning against the wall with his eyes turning upwards.)

They now looked in on the boathouse proper. There were a couple of peeling dinghies pulled up onto the concrete slipway and – wonderful to see – an ancient steam cruiser about twenty-five feet long. This, though old, did not look in the least neglected. Its brasswork gleamed, its funnel glinted, the glass of its cabin sparkled, and the very oil winked on its engine.

This, more than anything else, encouraged Freddie to go round and locate an entrance.

Following the wall back past the first window, they found a pair of double doors on the further side, with a smaller entry for human access centred in the right-hand flap.

There was another notice, again in faded lettering. It simply said 'GO AWA'.

'What does zat mean?' enquired Bertrand. 'Va t'en?'

'Yes.'

'But we are not going to go awa?'

'No.'

'Bravo.'

Bertrand smiled sweetly at Freddie. He appeared to have come out of his trance, encouraged perhaps by the promise of warmth and shelter within. Freddie felt better too. He had liked the look of that steamboat. There was always, of course, the dismissive nature of the notice on the door, but somehow its bark seemed worse than its bite.

He knocked firmly on the door: waited; and knocked again. This was for politeness's sake. He somehow knew that there would be no immediate response. He motioned to Bertrand to follow him round to the little back window again. Here he gave a little series of raps at the glass, gently at first, and then a pane-rattling volley.

For a moment, it crossed his mind that the figure in the bed might be dead. Bertrand evidently had the same idea.

'That he might be defunct?' he asked.

But suddenly the shape in the bed turned over.

Encouraged, Freddie rapped again.

The shape sat up, proclaiming itself by its short grizzled hair and rough demeanour to be a man. The shape shook its fist and lay down again, pulling the bedclothes over its head.

Freddie rapped on.

The shape got up wearily and started pulling on a long dirty velvet smoking jacket over its sweater, gave Freddie a dirty look and walked heavily to the door.

The boys trudged round to the other side again, and waited. Finally, there being still no sign that the man was going to open up, Freddie banged at the door unrestrainedly.

'All right, all right,' shouted a furious voice within. 'Can't a man have a piss in his own house?'

The door was flung open with an exuberance that nearly tore it from its hinges, and the man popped a grizzled red head out into the rain.

'Not today, thank you,' he said, and popped back in again, shutting the door behind him.

The boys looked at each other. Normally Freddie would have been appalled at his own effrontery, but the rain had made him reckless. He applied himself once more to the knocker.

The door opened more slowly this time, and revealed the man full-figure, complete with smoking jacket and grimy corduroy trousers.

'One would have thought,' said the man, heavily, addressing the nearest tree, 'one would have thought that even in this age of declining literacy, a youth would be able to read a simple notice.'

'I'm sorry,' said Freddie, 'but we tried at the house. We're staying at Flagg Foot. Mrs Seathwaite wrote to my mother saying we could call round any time. I'm Freddie Pemberton and this is Bertrand Vallier.'

'Ah, the youth speaks,' said the man, 'the youth can explain everything.'

'Bertrand is French,' said Freddie.

The man sighed heavily.

'You had better come in if you're going to explain everything. I cannot stand explanations in a draught.'

Freddie and Bertrand climbed through the door and stood in the dim watery light. Bertrand ran to the steamboat exclaiming with pleasure.

'Ah, que c'est beau.'

'Your French friend, youth, seems to have more tact than you do.'

'I'm sorry,' said Freddie.

'Coffee or whisky?' enquired the man.

'Er coffee, please?'

'And for you, Monsieur le Navigateur?'

'Du café, s'il vous plaît,' said Bertrand.

The man went into the back room, leaving them alone in the boathouse.

Freddie walked over to the little steamer.

She was indeed a beauty – not much bigger than a large rowing boat but complete with cabin, boiler, long brass funnel and brass-rimmed instruments.

Bertrand seemed totally besotted with her, caressing the boiler and reading the instruments as though they were the loved one's eyes.

'He is incroyable,' he cried. 'He marches?'

Freddie did not know if he marched. He was slightly put out – and knew it was absurd to be so – by the boat's superior claim on Bertrand's attention. At the same time, one couldn't help being impressed by the thing.

The SV *Proserpine* – the name written in bright black letters on the bows – must have been built at the beginning of the century, but she had the look of a boat still very much in use.

'If we play our cards right,' Freddie said, 'we might be able to negotiate a voyage for ourselves.'

The man came back with two steaming mugs.

'Coffee,' he said. 'You won't mind if I don't join you? Coffee makes me fart.'

It was instant coffee, only just brought out, and something of a rarity in Freddie's house. While the boys sipped, the man took out a bottle of whisky from one of the lockers and helped himself to a glass. Freddie later discovered that at least half the lockers in the place – and there were many – contained bottles of whisky.

'On second thoughts,' said the man, 'better come into the other room. Warmer in there.'

'Here you are,' he said, pulling out the two straight-backed chairs, and tipping off books, map and the cat, as the boys followed him in, 'sit ye doon.'

'Thank you,' said Freddie.

'I have decided to forgive you your trespass, and the more contumelious crime of waking me up. You are strangers. Your friend is foreign to our shores. We must extend a welcome, hm, Hecate, and stifle our natural sense of outrage.'

He fondled the cat's ears.

'Welcome to Hell Hall,' he continued. 'You have probably noticed the emphasis on the Underworld here. Proserpine . . . Hecate . . . wait until you meet my wife! I am, incidentally, Seathwaite. Sebastian Seathwaite. An ill-omened name, Sebastian, don't you think? All those arrows. And you are Freddie and Bertrand? How nice. So young. What did you say you were doing here?'

'My mother's mother and your wife's mother were cousins by marriage, I think,' said Freddie.

He had worked out the speech in advance. Prepared for explanation.

'Of course,' said Mr Seathwaite, 'one would naturally wish to come up from . . .'

'Bedfordshire.'

'From Bedfordshire in order to pursue such a pressing, such an intimate connection.'

'Well, it wasn't quite like that,' said Freddie.

In spite of the fact that Mr Seathwaite seemed, on the face of it, so robustly eccentric, there was at the same time a slightly bullying quality about the man. Freddie's sensitivities had been sharpened in the best English schools.

'You disappoint me,' said Mr Seathwaite.

Yes, it was definitely there, thought Freddie. He's trying to show me up in front of Bertrand.

'Well, we really came up to . . . to . . .'

The shadow of violence in the man made him flounder as doubtless it was intended to do. Freddie wasn't so sure that they should have come in here.

'You came up for a holiday, perhaps? Your friend Bertrand wanted a change from horrid sunny France?'

'Non non non,' cried Bertrand, in protest at the enormity of the assumption.

'It was our mothers,' said Freddie, waving his hands to indicate the uselessness of opposition.

'Ah, the mothers. It is always the mothers.'

'She means well,' said Freddie, not liking to be disloyal, especially in front of this strange man, 'but it's just this place we're staying at. There's only goat's milk to drink, and nothing to do, and it's raining all the time and . . .'

'Always the mother.'

'The man seemed to go into a decline. The boys drank their coffee and gazed around the room.

Over the table there was indeed a picture of St Sebastian being pierced by arrows, a pair of rather natty drawers around his loins and a yearning expression on his

100

face – not at all like the expression on Tommy Haynes's when Susie Biddle accidentally unleashed her arrow in the Midsummer Day Pageant staged by the Women's Institute at home. It had struck Tommy in the buttock as he crouched puckishly beside the tableau and he'd made no end of a fuss. It was an incident etched forever in Freddie's memory, and doubtless in Tommy's too, if not his buttock.

The silence became oppressive, only broken by the sound of the cat sharpening its claws on a valuable-looking leather-bound volume on the floor.

'Do you live down here?' asked Freddie in a voice which came out too abruptly.

'None of your business,' said Mr Seathwaite.

'I'm sorry,' said Freddie.

'Don't be sorry. You are inquisitive; enquire. Do not necessarily expect an answer.'

'What do you do?' asked Freddie, challenged.

'Do?'

'Everybody did something, except Rollo.

'I mean . . . do you have a job?'

'Job?'

Freddie became desperate. He was losing face fast.

'I mean . . . how do you spend the day?'

'I mope.'

'Just . . . mope?'

'Mostly.'

Freddie did not think the man was serious.

'Like an owl?' he said.

'How like an owl, youth?'

'"The moping owl doth to the moon complain,"' he quoted.

'Rather like an owl. But I also complain to the sun, the stars, the wind, the rain, the hills, the dales, and naturally to the lake itself.'

101

'What do you complain about?'

'What is there not to complain about?'

Freddie was impressed by the man's capacity for gloom. There was something grand, romantic even, about it, although he still wasn't sure he liked him.

'Wordsworth liked glooms,' he said.

'It's a good name for such a wordy poet, isn't it?' said Mr Seathwaite dismissively. 'Words worth. Turds worth.'

Freddie relished the quip, wishing he could repeat it to Aitken if not to Gibbers. It seemed the height of wit. He felt encouraged to question further.

'Do you eat down here?' he asked.

'Mostly.'

'Do you cook?'

'I live on bread and whisky. Sometimes beer. It is a simple yet satisfying economy.'

'Would you like to share our packed lunch?'

'Why not?'

Freddie and Bertrand opened the greaseproof paper and laid out their offerings. Two cheese sandwiches, two pork pies, two oranges, two chocolate biscuits, and a message in Freddie's package inscribed in a round immature hand which said, 'Yours is poisoned.' He snaffled it before Mr Seathwaite saw it.

'Beer?' suggested Mr Seathwaite, and opened a locker labelled 'Shackle Pins' from which he extracted a quart bottle of brown ale.

He poured a trickle into their empty coffee cups, swilled them out, and filled them to the brim. With this, he topped up his glass from the whisky bottle, and they set to.

Just to make sure that Isobel's billet doux was only a jape, Freddie held back while Mr Seathwaite addressed himself to the pork pies which he pronounced were 'ambrosia', and almost seduced him from his spare

102

regime. He wolfed them both down at great speed, showing no ill effects.

Reassured, Freddie embarked on a sandwich, eating it with long teeth. He did not know quite what to make of the man. Was he serious, or pulling their legs, or drunk? What was all this about Hell Hall, why was he so gloomy, what was he doing with all his bits of wireless which he didn't seem inclined to talk about? His manner half aggressive, half humorous, his unwholesome habits of life, his reluctance to live in the grand and presumably comfortable house, all these things presented questions whose answers were as shrouded in mist as the far shore of the lake itself. Above all, where was Mrs Seathwaite? His references to her had been hardly those of a loving husband.

Mr Seathwaite belched and lay down on his truckle bed.

'And now,' he said, 'for a little sleep. I work best at night. Dusk is my reveille. You have heard the horn?'

'The siffle is formidable,' said Bertrand who, while not joining in, had followed the conversation closely.

'It sounds like a monster's mating cry,' said Freddie. 'Have you ever seen the monster?'

Mr Seathwaite shot him a beady glance.

'It is the lament of Proserpine for the lost sunlight,' he said. 'Let yourselves out. I will send for you in due course.'

As they trudged up the path towards the road – the rain had almost stopped and a sickly sun filtered through pale pennants of nimbus – they saw a tall woman hurrying down towards them dressed in a black mackintosh and black galoshes which she wore with considerable panache.

As she drew near, they were able to observe that she had a handsome face, dark glasses, dark hair curling under the brim of her hat, and from what one could only judge under the impeding weatherwear, a generous figure. Were women with generous figures generous with their figures? It was something else to ask Aitken.

The woman approaching stopped them warmly and began apologizing.

'You must be Freddie,' she said, 'and you, Bertrand. I'm Elspeth Seathwaite.'

'How do you do?' said Freddie.

He could not imagine a more incongruous partner for the slovenly mariner below – except perhaps for a certain brooding quality in the fine dark eyes glimpsed behind the glasses.

'You must think me so rude,' she said. 'I was halfway up a ladder doing some curtains. Of course I heard the bell, but I thought it was one of those tiresome . . .'

She had a habit, Freddie learned, of letting sentences trail off wordlessly if she wasn't really interested in them.

'And then, of course, I suddenly had a qualm. I looked up your mother's letter and realized you were here. So I rang Flagg Foot and they said you'd set off in this direction. Anyway here you are. Have you had any lunch? You must be starving.'

'We've had our sandwiches, actually.'

'Well, come on in and have a chocolate or something. Do you like ping-pong? Vous jouez au ping-pong, Bertrand?'

'Ah oui.'

'Capital. We've got a table in the attic. Such a pity my nieces aren't here. They're staying with friends at the moment. They'll be back in a couple of . . .'

There was something attractive about her long legs and her abstracted manner, particularly the legs. She couldn't seem to keep her eyes off Bertrand. Freddie felt a stab of jealousy. At this rate, he thought, he was going to have as many punctures as bally Sebastian.

They followed the woman up the drive to the big granite house. Even though they were now proper visitors, there still seemed something slightly forbidding about it, or, if not forbidding, melancholy as though in a condition of lament.

'Here we are,' said Mrs Seathwaite, throwing open the front door. 'I expect you're jolly well soaked. I'll show you to where to put your things.'

The hall smelt of polish and flowers. She led them into a little cloakroom at the back where she hung up their weatherproofs and haversacks over a hot pipe. Then she ushered them into the drawing room where a fire, feathery with ash, smouldered under a half-gnawed blackened log, a grandfather clock tocked, and everything appeared to have been perfectly chosen and then screwed down into place.

'What a nice room,' said Freddie.

'But yes,' said Bertrand, his Gallic gallantry switching on like a lighthouse now this pretty Seathwaite was in the offing, 'je vous complimente, Madame.'

'That's jolly decent of you, Bertrand,' she said.

Freddie felt another stab. After all, he'd said it first. Why was the woman singling out Bertrand for gratitude? Bertrand was his. And yet, he had to admit, there was something very attractive about her.

Out of the concealing weatherproof, she wore a dark blue dress with a white collar; nothing much to write home about; but the general effect was awfully charming.

She still kept on the dark glasses. He wondered whether she kept them on all the time; whether she kept them on in bed.

There he went again. Why did he have to think about bed on the slightest pretext? Here she was, a perfectly nice woman offering them chocolates, and he had to take her clothes off.

Mrs Seathwaite didn't have thoughts like that.

She looked so perfectly composed. Her elegant legs moved with such certainty, and all her graceful actions and expressions somehow threw into relief the exciting-ness of what lay below, the undiscovered woman-country to whose bourne travellers kept returning and returning. From the waist down, they are centaurs, King Lear assured one. And yet it was axiomatic, at least according to Freddie's mother, that women were finer creatures. They did not have base instincts. They did not have erections. Their neat little cushions were not influenced by horny thoughts. One had to be worthy of them. They frowned on masturbation. That was why it was easier to make love to a boy – easier, of course, but not finer. The fine thing was to feel horny, and do nothing. The opposite of war when the fine thing was to feel shit scared and do everything. Why did the whole thing, the hole thing as Aitken put it, have to be so difficult?

Mrs Seathwaite went out to make some coffee, leaving them with the promised chocs – a large box of Suchard. The centres were just the sort Freddie liked – fudges, truffles and nut clusters rather than the despicable fruit creams. He ate four.

The Seathwaites seemed to have everything anybody could want.

Deciding that five chocs would overstep the bounds of good guestliness, he got up and wandered round to the piano. His eyes had been drawn to it as soon as they came in, but chocolates came first; besides, one didn't rush at people's pianos.

It lay across the far end of the room, its keyboard nearest the window with a vase of fuchsia standing on a small lace cloth beside a photograph in a silver frame of a rather good-looking young man in uniform on it; a brother or something no doubt.

Freddie opened the piano's lid reverently. He knew it was going to say Bechstein.

When he touched the chord of A Major, Mozart's favourite key, it was like driving a Rolls Royce – not that he'd ever driven anything except the Triumph in the drive at home when Rollo was out – but one heard a lot about it. Willoughby's father had a Bentley and Caradoc's had a prewar Silver Ghost and they went on about them as if they were Apollo's own fiery-footed chariots.

He sat down and played 'Hereford' by S. S. Wesley:

'Oh Thou who camest from above
The fire celestial to impart,
Kindle a flame of sacred love
On the mean altar of my heart.'

Mrs Seathwaite came in with the coffee while he was playing the last F Major chord and thinking about the mean altar of his heart.

'That was good, Freddie.'

'Bravo,' said Bertrand.

'I'm sorry,' said Freddie, 'do you mind me playing? I'm not very good actually. I mostly play just hymns.'

'It needs playing,' said Mrs Seathwaite. 'I believe it's good for it. And hymns must be specially good for it. Would you like coffee now or will you play some more?'

'Coffee, please.'

'Black for you, Bertrand?'

'Wiz milk, please, if it is not got.'

'He means goat,' said Freddie.

'Go-oh-oh-oh-ote,' said Bertrand.

'That's jolly good, Bertrand. Wish I could speak French as well as you speak English.'

After the coffee, Mrs Seathwaite offered to show them round the house.

'Yes, please,' said Freddie, observing that rain was

starting to fall again, slanting across the lawn beyond the French windows. 'That is, if you can spare the time.'

'Of course, I can,' said Mrs Seathwaite, 'it's the least I can do after not answering the door like that. I'm afraid Bertrand will have got a jolly dim impression of Lakeland hospitality.'

Bertrand smiled at her angelically. His smile had the effect of lighting up what in repose could seem an almost sulky expression. Stab, stab.

Mrs Seathwaite took them into the hall again from which the grand staircase climbed towards a distant skylight, flanked by baronial portraits.

'Are they Seathwaites?' asked Freddie.

'I should say so,' said she. 'Stuffy bunch, aren't they? This is the . . .'

A gleaming mahogany table flanked by bowlegged chairs and set with two heavy silver candlesticks under a chandelier which winked back the grey daylight in silver sparkles suggested to Freddie the dining room of the Veneerings. There was money in this house, very different from the eking-out (his mother's favourite game was Economy) which pervaded his own home. He had always wished he could live in a house like this, even if it didn't feel exactly homey.

Mrs Seathwaite showed them a billiard room with cues all neatly ranked in their case ready for brandy-and-cigar time.

'Do you play?' she asked.

'I've got a table at home,' said Freddie, 'but it's a miniature. This one's more like our croquet lawn.'

She laughed.

'And you, Bertrand, you play?'

'Bien sûr.'

'We must all have a game jolly soon. Cannon and kiss and . . .'

She led them along the corridor to the Gun Room in which she unlocked a cupboard and showed them half a dozen shotguns of various sizes from 12-bore to .410, two rifles, and an elephant gun – all with quantities of cartridges and ammunition, all neatly stacked in labelled drawers.

She gave them a tour of the fishing-rods, and flourished neat little tins with hinged Perspex lids full of gaudy flies.

As much as the wildness of the country outside, the vastness of the lake and the looming hugeness of the mountains, this glimpse of a feudal manner of life impressed Freddie's southern sensibilities. This was a foreign country of which he would have liked to have been a native.

She showed them model boats, intricate yachtlets fully rigged, even a little meths-driven steamer, baby sister of *Proserpine* in the boathouse.

She took them upstairs and opened bedroom doors, all comfortably and expensively furnished, with carafes of water and silver biscuit tins by the beds. Freddie peeped inside one of the canisters and found a little nest of crisp digestives.

The whole house seemed to be waiting for someone.

One door she did not open, and naturally Freddie asked what it was.

'Oh, that,' she said, 'just a spare room. It's in a bit of a mess at the moment. That was where I was doing the curtains when you called.'

Freddie had the impression that she didn't want to pursue the subject.

They climbed up at last to the landing under the skylight.

'I'm afraid it's a bit bare up here,' she said. 'We don't have so many guests nowadays, nor the staff come to that.'

She opened a door in a dividing wall, leading towards the back of the house. A little row of doors led off it.

'These used to be the servants' bedrooms,' she said. 'And this,' opening another door, 'this leads to the attics and the famous ping-pong room.'

They mounted a small circular stairway, opened a final door, and emerged into a long low room furnished only with a full-size table tennis set (Freddie's own one at home was inevitably smaller), and a latched chest full of bats and ping-pong balls.

'There you are,' said Mrs Seathwaite. 'That door at the end leads to the attic. Look around if you like but mind where you walk. Now I have to finish something downstairs. When you've had enough, come down and we'll arrange another day for you to come over. Next time we'll have a proper meal.'

She smiled at them – at Bertrand slightly longer than at him, Freddie thought, but it would be churlish to resent it – and went out, closing the door behind her.

'Eh bien,' said Freddie, vernacularly, 'ça va.'

'Ah oui,' said Bertrand. 'It is good egg.'

'What d'you want to do? Ping-pong or attic?' asked Freddie.

'Le ping-pong,' replied Bertrand, firmly.

Freddie had the feeling that Bertrand would be rather good, and so it proved. He darted about in a theatrical manner, hitting winners from impossible returns.

Freddie did not particularly like winning but he hated being beaten. The score went against him 15–21, 14–21 and, lamentably, 10–21.

'I've had enough,' he said at last, 'come on, let's go down.'

And he put his bat back in the chest and went to the door. He turned the handle but it wouldn't open. He tried it again, budging it with his shoulder. It refused to respond, turning round and round uselessly in his hand.

Freddie's lively imagination sprang into action with a myriad possibilities. Like the three old ladies stuck in the lavatory, 'nobody knew they were there'. They would be locked here forever like the girl in the Mistletoe Bough, found in skeleton order years and years later. The only person who was aware of them was Mrs Seathwaite, and maybe she had fallen off her ladder and broken her neck, or suffered amnesia, or had simply gone mad.

Or . . . there was a lunatic in the attic, a deranged brother or sister, who only ate human flesh.

Freddie turned white-faced to Bertrand, his upper lip all over the place.

'Nous somme perdus,' he said dramatically, drawing on memories of Racine's *Hippolyte*, and throwing in an 'oh ciel'.

Bertrand came over and tried the door for himself.

'Ça ne fait rien,' he said, remaining infuriatingly calm. 'We will make a reconnaissance. Perhaps there is a door in other part.'

Freddie thought, the more he saw of Bertrand the less he knew him. It wasn't the fact that he was foreign and had a funny way with English, there was something curiously private about him. However, his imperturbability had a soothing effect.

There was nothing for it but to head for the attic. Though calmer, Freddie was now beset by fresh imaginings. He had always been scarily fascinated by the thought of ghosts and poltergeists. A book called *Haunted Britain* was a constant source of reference. His brother had been to Borley Rectory and a brick had appeared from nowhere when he was walking in the orchard near the flattened ruin of the house, landing at his feet like an awful warning.

111

But this was a bit near the mark. Perhaps Hell Hall was haunted by something that would turn your hair white overnight. It had to be something like that, otherwise why would Mr Seathwaite want to call it Hell Hall?

The room that was disclosed when they opened the door looked harmless enough. Lit by a cobwebby window, the low-ceilinged space was occupied by very much the same sort of things that cluttered the attic at home. Trunks, cases, a tuck-box or two, chairs with broken backs awaiting eternally postponed repair, a tea-chest full of old papers . . . there was nothing here to disturb or unsettle . . . by day . . . with a companion . . .

They progressed into the next section, this one illuminated by a small dusty skylight, still searching for an alternative exit.

This room was spookier. There was a dressmaker's dummy for a start which Freddie took for a real person as he rounded a corner bravely in front of Bertrand. He was already feeling ashamed of his funk – after all, they could always break the door down – but the dummy made him give a little yodel of surprise.

Bertrand came up and did a little dance with it, which made them both feel better, and they passed on to the rocking horse – badly in need of a new tail – which squeaked like a banshee, and a doll's house which reminded him of a ghost story he had read.

There was a train set which didn't work, a broken banjo, a couple of teddy bears, and a number of old tennis rackets, a pile of old photograph albums, a postcard collection, and an Edwardian Birthday Book full of the sprightly apophthegms of the long-dead.

'"My Greatest Happiness . . . a cigar on the lawn after breakfast. My Greatest Unhappiness . . . listening to Kitty playing Ravel,"' read Freddie.

Finally, at the end of the room, among a chamber-pot

commode and a couple of washstands, there was a great mahogany tallboy full of old clothes and fancy dress. As they approached it, something rather eerie happened. Its great door swung silently open.

Even Bertrand looked rather pained, and Freddie whinnied, expecting a long-dead corpse to drop out of it. However, nothing emerged except a couple of moths, and the boys began to examine the contents.

There were long dresses, and pierrot costumes, there was a magician's cape and top-hat, there were pirate's rigs and a clown's kit, there were swords, wands, walking sticks and blunderbusses. Every conceivable costume and contrivance for Bal Masqué or domestic charade seemed to be catered for. Bertrand selected a moth-eaten lion outfit and Freddie found a striped blazer with OULTC and a pair of crossed tennis rackets on its top pocket. They strutted about, admiring their reflections in a dusty mirror.

Just at this moment Freddie had the curious sensation that they were being watched.

Perhaps it was a very faint draught that made its passage felt, twitching the feathers of a boa that he had hung up on the doorhandle, twirling the dust in the intermittent pale tendrils of sunlight. Bertrand also sensed something, for he stopped searching for the lion's head.

They both looked round.

Mrs Seathwaite was standing under the skylight looking at Bertrand, ashen-faced. Freddie's first potty-trained instinct was guilt. What had they done wrong? His second reaction was puzzlement. How and why had she come in so quietly?

With a great effort, Mrs Seathwaite composed herself, 'I . . . I'm sorry,' she said. 'Bertrand looked so awfully like someone. I couldn't . . .'

'We were just looking round,' said Freddie rather

113

shamefacedly, embarrassed at having been overseen and not quite certain of wrong-doing.

'Quite right too,' said Mrs Seathwaite, more naturally, 'so you jolly well should. I say, you know, you don't have to stop.'

But the boys were taking off their costumes and returning them to the tallboy. Somehow they didn't feel like fooling around any more. They followed her back into the ping-pong room. The door to the landing was wide open.

'The door was stuck,' Freddie said. 'We couldn't get it open.'

'What a chump I am. I should've told you. It's a frightful rotter, that door. You have to persevere. It always works in the end. I say, I'm frightfully sorry. You must have felt like one of Bluebeard's prisoners.'

How wet of him not to be able to get a stupid door open, thought Freddie. All the same, there was something odd about the way she had looked at Bertrand.

'Who won the ping-pong?' she asked over his shoulder as they went downstairs.

'Bertrand did,' said Freddie. 'He was too good for me.'

He wished people didn't always have to ask who won – winning wasn't important, according to Mother. It was how you played the game. Though, come to think of it, he'd played the game like a spastic teaspoon.

'You must come again and have your revenge,' said Mrs Seathwaite.

'That'd be nice.'

'You ought to come and have tea. What about Tuesday? There's a super baker in Ambleside who does cream cakes and doughnuts and things . . .'

Freddie's mouth watered. Rationing had only stopped a few years ago, and even now they still had margarine instead of butter at school, and very often at home as well. And of course at Flat Foot, inevitably, they had bright yellow margarine which tasted of cricket bat oil and felt furry on your tongue. It was now Saturday. They would have two more days of Flat Foot cooking in the interim to sharpen their appetites.

And yet . . . there was something about the house that made him wary. Besides there was the monster to be monitored. And the strange Mr Seathwaite might come up with an offer of a trip in the steamer. And he didn't really want to share Bertrand with all these people just yet.

'We'd love to sometime,' he said. 'It's just that we may be going on a boat trip . . .'

He made a gesture with his head to indicate the boathouse.

'It's all a bit in the air at the moment,' he said.

Mrs Seathwaite's face clouded. Bertrand shot an enigmatic look at Freddie.

'You can jolly well do what you like,' said Mrs Seathwaite. 'I don't want to stop you. If he,' here she gestured contemptuously as if mimicking Freddie, 'if he has asked you to join him in his boat, that's fine. I can see the attraction. I think it's smelly, uncomfortable and highly dangerous. I don't know what your mothers would think of the idea.'

It was a strange outburst.

'Dangerous?' queried Freddie, ever susceptible to alarm.

'If the safety valve sticks, or the water pump packs up, there's nothing to stop it exploding. Oh, I don't want to put you off. It's historic all right. But a trip in a boat in which Edward the Seventh once sailed doesn't really make up for being scattered over the lake like fishbait.'

'Oh,' said Freddie.

'I say, I hope I haven't put you off.'

'N-not at all,' said Freddie.

115

'What d'you think, Bertrand?' he asked the French boy who was staring at him with his great dark-blue-rimmed blue eyes.

'As you like.'

'No, c'est comme tu veux,' said Mrs Seathwaite.

Freddie could feel a sulk coming on. Why was she calling Bertrand 'tu' when he, Freddie, had only reached it after three days? Annoyance made him stick to his guns.

'I think we should go if we're asked. It would be rude not to.'

'Oh, rude,' said Mrs Seathwaite contemptuously, gesturing boathousewards again, 'that's a good argument, that is. He knows all about that.'

For all her tragic air, there was a strength about the woman.

Bertrand unexpectedly chipped in: 'He has not said us which day.'

Freddie suddenly wondered what his mother was doing, whether she was thinking of him up there on the salmony River Annan where the maids did your unpacking for you and the trumps thumped all night in the card room.

He waved his hands hopelessly.

'That's settled, then,' said Mrs Seathwaite. 'Come to tea on Tuesday, and we'll see what sort of show the landlubbers can put on to entertain you.'

'Goodbye, Freddie.'

She kissed him on the cheek with cool affection.

'Au revoir, Bertrand,' she said, and gave the French boy what, to the casual observer, would have seemed an identical little peck, but to Freddie's monitoring eye was at least an inch closer to the mouth – and then repeated it on the other side as well . . .

'That's because he's French,' she said, noting Freddie's look of surprise. 'They do it on both sides, you know.'

Freddie blushed. He didn't think that was what Aitken meant when he talked about French kissing. He noticed that Bertrand was blushing too. Like a little Cherubino, he thought, recalling last term's visit to the opera with the School Musical Society.

15

They were late for high tea, to the delight of Isobel.

High tea was sharp at six, and they arrived back at quarter past, having stopped on the way back to watch an intriguing set of ripples. It was so easy to imagine the smooth serpentine snout that would stick from such a wriggliness in the water. But there was no point in telling Isobel about it, even if they hadn't sworn each other to secrecy. Isobel's smooth little snout was so stuck in the air with smug glee that she out-monstered any monster you could imagine.

'You won't half catch it,' she said to Freddie, squirming with malice.

Mr Aylott came in with a face of thunder.

'I'll say it once and I'll say it once only. I don't want Mrs Aylott fussed. If you can't turn up in time for meals, there'll be no meals, simple as that. And if you don't like, you can luke for somewhere else to stay.'

'Sorry, Mr Aylott,' said Freddie, and then thinking to show solicitude, 'How are the goats?'

'Worse,' said Mr Aylott in a rage. 'T'vet said you ought to be ashamed of yourself. He said we ought to try giving you toilet paper to your tea, and I had a bloody good mind to. Nowt but trouble, you are.'

Tea consisted of two greasy little rashers of bacon with two tinned tomatoes swimming along beside them like jellyfish. It was only a marginal improvement on Bronco. The boys picked at their plates. The promised Seathwaite gâteaux seemed infinitely attractive. What had he been thinking of to be so maidenly about them?

'He's only mad at you because they can't have babies,' said Isobel, appearing with the teapot. 'They try and try but I think he's got a low sperm count. He's kind of mean, don't you think?'

She was trying to suck up after her gloating. Freddie was struck by the research that went into all her findings.

'There's not much you don't know, is there?' he said. 'How is it you never learned any manners?'

She stuck her tongue out as she took away their plates. He did not associate Isobel with the female sex.

After tea, just as they were preparing to go down and have a monster watch, it started peeing down again, so they decided to leave it for tomorrow.

They wandered into the Res Lounge where Freddie twiddled the exhausted wireless while Bertrand thumbed through back numbers of the *Lakeland Courier*. Against all expectation, the radio suddenly emitted a screech and a burst of impenetrable German.

Bertrand looked up quickly.

'Not zat,' he said, 'I not like zat. I hear too much of zat when I am little.'

'You were in Germany?' asked Freddie, puzzled.

'Ah no. The Germans were in France. They take my oncle and shoot him, pouf.'

Freddie did not know what to say. He had not thought that Bertrand would have experienced at first hand a war which, apart from the odd stray bomb in the farmer's field, and a doodlebug in a nearby beechwood, had been for him very much an arm's-length affair.

He turned the dial quickly, not knowing what to say and hoping for harpsichord music (he had, with a boy called Beadle, put drawing pins into the felt hammers of the superannuated piano in the Rehearsal Room of the School Theatre in order to produce this favourite effect),

119

but all he could find was 'Bimbo, Bimbo, what you going to do-io?' on the Hilversum wavelength.

He wanted to ask Bertrand about the war but he sensed that Bertrand did not want to talk about it. All the time, he was conscious of the desire growing in him like a horse-radish.

He hurried to the bedroom to find his Wordsworth. He could think of nothing else that would effectively counter such stirrings of carnality.

Returning, he sat himself down and diligently turned the pages in search of his pencil mark. Ah yes! Here it was.

> 'Wisdom and Spirit of the Universe!
> Thou Soul that art the eternity of thought,
> That givest to forms and images a breath
> And everlasting motion, not in vain
> By day or star-light thus from my first dawn
> Of childhood didst thou intertwine for me
> The passions that build up our human soul;
> Not with the mean and vulgar works of man . . .'

The words swam before his eyes, wriggling monsters of meaning that seemed to mean nothing. It was no good. He was going to have to go and do a mean and vulgar work of man in the lav.

Bertrand looked at him curiously as he hurried out, but made no comment.

This time Freddie remembered to close the window.

16

Freddie woke late next morning. It was just as well. He couldn't have another toss because he'd used up his ration last night. He lay in bed thinking of Bertrand, while the little alarm clock his mother had given him clicked on past getting-up time.

He thought how golden brown and soft Bertrand was, with a low light voice which didn't sound exactly broken. There were no discernible shag-spots, nor bristles on the lip, but then he was only sixteen, and some boys didn't start till late, like Purvis who had an undropped testicle, worse luck.

And then he thought about Mrs Seathwaite with her preoccupied air and generous bosom. Aitken had categorized bosoms for the benefit of the Junior Common Room: Knobbers, Bobbers, Droopers, and Super-Droopers. Mrs Seathwaite's were very definitely in the latter bracket. What would it be like to swing like a grasshopper on the well-filled cornucopia of her brassière?

'Viens, Freddie,' said Bertrand, 'we must not be retarded for breakfast.'

It was encouraging to note that he was taking some responsibility for things. They dressed hurriedly, Freddie trying not to dwell on Bertrand's shirt-fringed thighs, and ran down the corridor to be in time for the cornflakes.

'Rapture,' said Freddie. 'Cow's milk again.'

As they spooned hungrily away, Freddie checked the weather. A flat low grey cloud sat over the lake without doing anything except obliterate the hilltops. Freddie had assumed that it was raining, but the cloud was too inert even to do that. It reminded him of 'Gamma' Spofforth, a boy one year his senior with whom he had had to share a study for a term.

Isobel came in with some boiled eggs.

'Bonjour, chéri,' she said to Bertrand, ignoring Freddie, 'qu'est ce que tu veux faire aujourd'hui? Mes cuisses t'attendent.'

'This egg's bad,' said Freddie.

She craned over him, brushing him with her knobbers.

'Perfectly OK,' she pronounced. 'You're the rotten one.'

'Oi,' a voice shouted at her from the kitchen.

'Let's get the boat again,' said Freddie, 'and go back to where we saw the torment of the water.'

'D'accord,' said Bertrand. 'We shall make a method scientifique.'

Jackie selected *Daffodil* for them this time, saying he reckoned *Lucy* ought to have a rest, and he'd tan their hides if they so much as knocked a spot off her bottom.

The 'Gamma Spofforth' sky invested the surface of the water with its own grey lethargy. Not a ripple disturbed the surface, even the flies seemed to have taken the day off, and only the crows wallowing about in the distant fields indicated any kind of avian activity.

Bertrand rowed first, and Freddie sat in the stern trying not to look up his short trouser legs while he heaved away at the oars. The hamlet receded, the watery expanse surrounded, the rowlocks squeaked in a dirge; not only was there no chance of sighting a monster, there wasn't even a minnow to break the pervading lifelessness.

His thoughts kept on turning back to Hell Hall. At least that had been unexpected. If he could not – and he could not – tamper with Bertrand's springs of life, there was precious little else to do pending the appearance of the

122

reluctant monster but ponder the strange deportment of these cousins of cousins by marriage.

'Tiens,' said Bertrand, 'we are arrived.'

The boathouse where they had had their lunch on the first day hove into view. They landed and, sat where they had sat before. It was too early for lunch. They looked out on the water waiting for a swirl.

They waited ten minutes, and then Freddie got out another miniature, this time Drambuie. The flicker of cordial instilled a tiny measure of, if not optimism, at least animation. Freddie had counted his miniatures before leaving. There were only six left. At this rate, it would mean some very bleak days in week 2.

'So, come on, Bertrand,' he said, as they licked the last droplet from the tiny mouth, 'what about this scientific method of yours?'

'We take a line,' said Bertrand, pointing straight across the lake to the edge of a coppice, 'and we traverse, and then we move ten metres and we traverse again, and so some more, etcetera. The one who does not row shall take notes on the phénomènes.'

He undid a pocket of his coat, and showed a small exercise book.

'It sounds a bit, well, not very exciting,' Freddie said doubtfully.

'It is not very exciting. That is the essence of the méthode scientifique.'

'Oh,' said Freddie.

'But it is very exciting, no?, when we discover the monster and can say exactly where with our carte. And besides, we have nothing else to do.'

'You have reason,' said Freddie.

They consulted the Ordnance Survey, decided which line they would take first, and stepped back into the boat.

Freddie grasped the oars while Bertrand took up his pencil and notebook like a shorthand typist.

After an hour, they had traversed the lake four times. Bertrand's little book contained the precise hour and minute of each sweep, and its precise location was marked in pencil on the map; but there was no comment to add. Not even a hint of an out of place plop.

'Time for lunch, I votes,' said Freddie, as they neared the further side for the second time.

There was a little natural jetty here with a grassy lawn fringed by trees. It looked a good spot for a picnic, almost as though it had been cleared and tended for the comfort and ease of monster hunters.

The packed lunch today consisted of squashy tomatoes, corned beef sandwiches, seedcake, and oranges again.

'What is this seatcake?' asked Bertrand, wrinkling his nose in French fashion.

'Seed cake. Seed.'

'I do not like seed. Seed is for birds. Oof.'

He threw his seedcake into the water.

A couple of ducks, one of the only signs of life so far all day, obediently swam round the corner and devoured it.

The seedcake seemed to have put Bertrand into a bate. He stamped up and down the clearing, muttering: 'Seedcake . . . je m'en fiche de seedcake, what am I doing in this seedy place with these cakey peoples and these rains and . . . tiens . . .'

He had stopped and was looking down at what Freddie had thought was a flat rock at the far end of the clearing near the water's edge.

'What is it, Bertrand?'

Freddie stood up in mid-cake, and went over to him. He was staring at a simple inscription on the rock. It read: J. S. August 1940.

They both stood in silence. Freddie, with his half-eaten

cake in his hand, trying to imagine what had happened to whom.

As if trying to take his mind off the misfortune, Bertrand glanced across the water, away from the stone, and suddenly stiffened.

'What is it, Bertrand?'

'The water . . . over there . . .'

Freddie followed his pointing finger and, sure enough, the same raised swirliness was racing across the still surface like the ripple from a huge invisible splash. It passed close by, heading down the lake towards Flat Foot, gently rocking the grasses at the water's edge.

'Gosh,' said Freddie.

'I will write it in the book,' said Bertrand. 'But, alas, a ripple is not a monster. Can you see an énorme head?'

They peered earnestly about but no enormity was to be viewed.

'It is better than nothing but it is not much better,' said Bertrand. 'Come, let us recommence.'

They spent the rest of the day rowing to and fro across the lake without further contact. By four o'clock Freddie was growing very bored indeed of the method scientific. His hands were becoming blistered and his bottom was sore from *Daffodil*'s hard thwart. Bertrand seemed to derive some strange zeal from the quest, like Jack Hawkins hunting a submarine.

Freddie had read *The Cruel Sea*. It was considered very racy. And his uncle had taken him out from school to see the film. He could remember the captain's obstinate refusal to stop searching, in the teeth of all the evidence. So it was with Bertrand. It was magnificent. But after all, this was not the war.

'Come, Bertrand,' he said at last. 'We shall be late if we don't get our skates on.'

He never thought he would be so grateful for the call of Flat Foot fare.

17

The next day and the next passed in almost exactly the same manner.

Only details differed. The cloud was higher and intermittently sent down a dusting of moisture so light you could hardly call it rain. A lunatic with an outboard motor launch came whizzing by them from further up the lake, probably a tripper with a trailer. Jackie had told them there were no other boatyards on Ettenwater.

The man's wife sat bolt upright with a scarf around her hair and a glass of what looked like gin and tonic in her hand.

Apart from the wash of the launch, which nearly upset them, there were no strange ripples. They traversed their appointed stretches nine times, stopping for lunch at a place where a little beck flung itself ardently into the complaisant water of the lake.

Freddie liked the ardent stream. It was he who chose the spot. He would have liked to fling himself ardently onto someone, but no one seemed to want it.

By the end of the second day, he was totally fed up with boats, monsters, French boys, hills of the north, sex, sandwiches, water, clouds, ducks, midges, crows, cattle, method scientific, and for that matter method completely bally random and hopeless. All he wanted to do was go home, play the piano, knock a tennis ball against the garage door, and look at Hildegard's hairy armpits while she made apple soup.

Tea, however, for a change, was rather good; fried eggs and fried potatoes with fresh field mushrooms. Even

Bertrand was impressed. The goats were still off their milk so there was cow's milk again to go with the Brown Betty teapot.

Revived by this unexpected gastronomic turn-up, Freddie suggested a walk afterwards to How Rock – the place where the book had said that human sacrifices used to take place.

'I will ask Mrs Aylott if she has some scraps to spare in case the monster has lost his taste for maidens,' he told Bertrand.

Mrs Aylott proved to be unexpectedly forthcoming. Either she was usually too immersed in her labours to lift her head – pale, slightly heavy, but rather pretty features when you got to look at them, with luxuriant brown hair curled back in a bun – or Mr Aylott exerted a negative effect upon her when he was around. It was a trait that Freddie had noticed before among married couples.

'Walking?' she said. 'You can borrow Mr Aylott's boat. He's over in Whitehaven seeing the bank. He'll be staying the night. He won't mind this once. Be careful now.'

This was a rare privilege, since Aylott had impressed upon them the sacrosanctity of his vessel. It was lighter and faster than any of Jackie's.

Freddie had blistered hands, so Bertrand rowed, shipping his oars with practised panache as they slid beside the grassy rootiness of the How Rock mooring.

> 'O say, did you know of that jolly young waterman
> Who at Blackfriars Bridge used for to ply,
> He feathered his oars with such skill and dexterity
> Charming each heart and delighting each eye,'

chanted Freddie, music by Charles Dibdin.

How Rock was a lump of stone encrusted with lichen and tufts of grass sprouting irregularly like Biddle Major's attempt at a moustache. Beside it was a grassy space of perhaps fifty yards circumference.

There was nothing to indicate human sacrifice.

'Put the food near the rock, on the lake side,' said Freddie. 'It's a pity you're not a beautiful maiden. We could tie you to the rock and leave you overnight like Andromeda.'

Bertrand looked beautiful enough to whet any monster's appetite.

'Very droll,' said Bertrand.

They placed the food on top of the knobbly stone in a little sacrificial niche seemingly scooped out for the role, where it sat like a strange fungal efflorescence: bulgy sausage roll, sticky glistening bacon, and death cap cheese.

They began the monster talk.

'Will he come soon?'

'I think he will come when we are not watching. He will know when we are watching.'

'What will he look like?'

'He will be green.'

'He will not be bright green, I think.'

'He will be dull green.'

'There will be warts and shaggers. And slime.'

'Will it be a long monster?'

'At least forty feet. That is to say about twelve metres.'

'There will be undulations?'

'Three or four humps at least.'

'What will it smell of?'

'Death.'

'Does the monster eat people?'

'Only when it is desperate. Otherwise it prefers sausage roll.'

'We should pray now to the monster to make it smile upon us.'

'O monster,' Freddie looked out across the forlorn waste of water, and prayed with all his heart. 'O monster, come to us, eat our sausage roll, and we will worship you as is fitting. Come creaming across the lake in your glorious majesty, or simply pop up without ceremony, it is all one to us, we only crave thy monstrous presence. Your turn now.'

'O monstre, fier et puissant,' began Bertrand, but Freddie cut him short.

'It's an English monster,' he said. 'It can't understand all that froggy babbling.'

'He understand frog if he live in a lake,' said Bertrand, unenraged, 'but if you wish I will give him my best rosbif. O monster, you are the best things that ever happen in my vacances. I have seened you in my dream. Now come truly, and make us the honneur of your appearances. I am sorry this English saucisse en croûte is so red and pepper and in texture like eating a tennis ball. But it is all we have. It is our own food. Take it please now or if necessary when we removed ourselves.'

'Not bad,' said Freddie, 'though you got in a bugger's muddle with your tenses. But I don't suppose the monster really cares too much about tenses. He probably only wants the drift of things.'

Pity Bertrand wouldn't understand the drift joke either.

'What does the monster do all day?' asked Bertrand.

'He sleeps under the whelming tide,' said Freddie, 'in a cavern decorated with bones. He dozes fitfully and thinks of the days when the lake was stiff with monsters. He remembers his youth and how he played boulder polo with his brothers and sisters. He is the last monster now. He thinks of his solitude. He is sad and angry.'

'Why does he not come out and crush the buildings in his anger?'

129

'He knows they would come with guns and destroy him.'

'He is a monster. Bullets would not derange him.'

'They would drop an atom bomb on him. He knows about these things. He feels the earth shaking in his cave of bones.'

Totally exhausted by nightfall, Freddie could feel the earth shaking in his cave of bones too. The fatigue made him almost rash enough to tell Bertrand that he thought he might be in love with him.

If I don't tell him now, he thought, I'll never do it, I don't care what he thinks of me.

But he still said nothing. Instead he plunged into a slumber as profound as the unfathomable depths of the lake itself – a slumber in which strange dreams rose and fell, and angel faces with muddy bodies danced beneath the waves and finny phalluses sported in the weed.

18

He woke to the familiar refrain of rattling windows and pattering rain, but he felt like a different person; his lake gloom gone; his view of Bertrand's sleeping head was not veiled by frustration but simply affectionate; the day ahead did not seem like another long haul, but an adventure.

As if echoing his mood, the door opened and Isobel appeared with a tray of tea and biscuits.

'Auntie thought you'd better have some tea. She said you looked all in last night. She hopes you're not sickening for something. But you're not, are you? You're just sickening.'

She retreated hastily as he threw his pillow at her.

As he sipped his tea, he thought about her, and Mrs Aylott, and women, and his mind came back to Mrs Seathwaite. Why had she looked at Bertrand so oddly in the attic? Aitken would have said it could only mean one thing. Freddie hoped that it wouldn't be so. He was intrigued by How Hall, and he loved the Bechstein, he wanted to go back there; but maybe she loved Bertrand too and would take him away from him.

Freddie had in his sixteen years encountered a number of embarrassing situations. There had been the matter of his Housemaster's wife and the desperate attack of squitters, and his great-aunt's priceless footstool that he'd sat on and broken, there had been the wet dream he'd had when staying with the Wicklows when Mrs Wicklow would insist on helping him make his bed, there had been

131

bogies hanging out at parties, and getting his sleeve-buttons caught in the dress of the girl at the Pony Club Dance, and the dog turd trodden into the Admiral's carpet when he'd been asked in with the carol singers, and the dreadful occasion when his mother's knicker elastic had broken and she'd stood there roaring with laughter with her pink bloomers on the pavement.

But none of his experiences had prepared him for the contentious role of jealous chaperone. He could hardly ask his hostess to keep her hands off his friend.

Bertrand opened an eye.

'No method scientific today, I think, Freddie.'

'It's all right. I don't mind. Maybe I overdid the rowing. They row at my school but I play cricket.'

It was a feeble excuse but Bertrand didn't seem to mind.

'Maybe we walk this morning,' he said.

'All right. We row this afternoon. This afternoon we find the monster.'

There was no Mr Leacock at breakfast, which was an added bonus, and Isobel served their poached eggs with almost embarrassing solicitude until you realized she was just overdoing it as usual.

After breakfast, they put on their coats and gumboots, collected their sandwiches, and headed for a track Freddie had noticed winding uphill from the lane that led towards Hell Hall.

They eased their haversacks and addressed themselves to the climb.

The path ascended through a copse, crossed a muddy track, and confronted them with a closed gate. Beyond it, the way led up and up through lumpy upland pasture dotted with grazing sheep.

Freddie hastily checked for bulls and rams, but Bertrand was already going over. Freddie picked up a stick and followed him, warily eyeing a couple of large sheep which warily eyed him back and finally tittuped out of the way as they passed.

They climbed on and on until, at the top of the last slope, the track led to the edge of a little tarn. To their left, the peaks rose ridge upon ridge to the hidden summit of Stickletop. To the right were rounder hills, also rising above them, covered with forest. Before them, between the shoulders of heathery slopes, they could see the shining water of another lake.

As they climbed, Freddie's spirits had correspondingly dropped. There was no one in sight. No cottage, not even a hut relieved the isolation of upland and stone wall. The great peaks on the horizon confirmed the solitude.

Freddie shivered. He had known, of course, that the Lakes were wild but he had never been anywhere quite so uncompromisingly manless. What would it be like to be up here at night . . . in a storm?

The showers which had accompanied them on the way up had temporarily abated, and great ragged curtains of cloud streamed across the window of the hills. A swirl of wind whirred in a standing rock.

What was it Turdsworth said:

'The ghostly language of the ancient earth'?

Perhaps there was something in it after all. This nature was strong stuff.

It made his furtive rubbings seem small and grubby, and yet, at the same time, he had been driven by something just as much as the clouds were driven. This must be nature too.

'I say, Bertrand,' he shouted above the wind, 'shall we go down? It's bally cold up here. I didn't put my sweater on. Let's find a place where we can have lunch and do a

133

spot of monster watching. It's going to rain like stink at any moment.'

Bertrand nodded. It was as usual impossible to tell exactly what he was thinking.

On their way down, they did indeed see a dreaded ram. It was standing alone beside a twisted thorn tree, its curly horns and great bag of balls seemingly made from the same hard weatherbeaten matter as the wind-polished hill itself.

It paused as they passed, and gazed at them, and Freddie gripped his stick, knowing it would be useless against that great butting Ionic column of a head, but Bertrand walked on unconcernedly – hero doubtless of a dozen encounters with bull chamois in the Alps – and the beast, as if in acknowledgement of the boy's charmed presence, reverted to its grazing without a further glance in their direction.

What made the beast so patient, Freddie wondered, as the rain started again, what did it have in mind under its tree? If he had a bag of balls like that it would weigh heavily upon him. He had enough trouble with his own small valise.

How different was this dignified ram from the ram of the favourite Junior Common Room ditty, 'The Ram of Derbyshire'.

> 'When the ram was young, sir,
> He had a stroke of luck,
> They left him in a field of ewes,
> And he gave them all a . . .'

How often had he, Freddie, led the chorus.

'I am worse than the animals,' he thought. 'I am the beast.'

'Courage,' said Bertrand, mistaking his grimace. 'Now we sit in a boathouse and drink cognac and eat Spam.'

134

However, the boathouse they had used before was on the other side of the lake, and they had to make do with a derelict sheepcote near the water's edge. Here they sat on a couple of stones, looking out on the water through the doorless lintel while the rain hosed across the surface.

Bertrand, typically dark horse, had brought a bottle of brandy with him in his luggage. His mother had told him to give it to Rollo, but he had thought he would leave it until his departure. And now he'd found a more urgent use for it at Flat Foot.

'Good egg, Bertrand.'

After lunch, they squelched unsteadily down the lake-side to How Rock – a walk of twenty minutes or so – to see how their offering had been received.

The food was gone.

They had placed it too high for a fox's thieving. Birds would have left some evidence – shit or crumbs. Squirrels would hardly have been tempted by the fibrous gristle.

There could, of course, have been a number of explanations, but it seemed quite clear to the boys that the miracle had occurred. The monster had answered their invitation.

They placed more food; the breakfast bacon, some black pudding they'd purchased at the little shop, and stale bread they'd seen the old woman about to throw away.

'Tonight,' said Bertrand, 'we come to watch. We come to catch the monster at his supper.'

Freddie was immediately thrown into a turmoil. He wanted, very much, to see the monster. On the other hand, it sounded as if it could be hairy. Monster or no monster, who knew what madman or wild creature would get jolly stroppy if disturbed in mid sausage-roll.

Half of Freddie, the nearly grownup half, the half

135

which in a couple of years would be leading a platoon of riflemen against terrorists in Cyprus – half of him knew there was no monster. But half of him was still a child, and the monster was as possible as a boggle under the bed.

'We come tonight?' asked Bertrand, staring at him with his cobalt-blue eyes.

'I expect so,' said Freddie. 'Got any more of that brandy?'

19

'Ooh, you've been drinking,' said Isobel, as she issued them each with a pale coil of tripe, 'you smell like a distillery. Gimme, gimme.'

To keep her quiet, they said they'd give her a drop after tea.

'That Leacock,' she told them, sitting on the edge of the sideboard and swinging her legs, 'that Leacock lent Uncle and Auntie some money. But Uncle's not going to be able to pay him back. Leacock's just waiting to move in. He's evil.'

'Oi,' came ringing down the corridor.

'Better go,' she said. 'Bottoms up and trousers down.'

'This girl is cuckoo,' said Bertrand.

As they were leaving to put more food on the rock and to wait as late as they dared (Mr Aylott had now returned) for the monster or whatever else it was to show up, Isobel reappeared in the hall. Freddie had forgotten his promise of a swig. She took a furtive suck from the bottle, and chewed a mint.

'Where are you going?'

'Secret.'

'Oooh, can I come?'

Freddie looked at Bertrand, an idea forming in his mind. Perhaps the monster really did prefer maidens.

'She might do as the sacrifice. Better than a sausage roll.'

'That's the nicest thing you ever said to me. What are you going to do?'

'Tie you to the Rock.'

'Yes, please.'

'You'll be smirking on the other side of your face if the monster comes.'

'Then you will have to rescue me, chéri,' she said to Bertrand. 'I shall naturally be clad in gauzy white.'

'We don't have any gauzy white,' said Freddie, crossly.

'I do,' she said. 'There's some old net curtains in the loft. I'll bring them along.'

Freddie grumbled about the delay but they waited for her.

They trudged along to the Rock in the dove-grey twilight, Bertrand in front, Isobel with her bundle of net, and Freddie bringing up the rear, walking among the trodden ways of everyone else's gumboots, with a bag of scraps in case Isobel got cold feet.

Freddie shivered when they arrived. The place did have a kind of eerie feeling about it after sundown.

Over the water, a light mist hovered in strange little clumps.

Isobel seemed unaware of the broodiness of the scene. She slipped off her dress before the boys could even turn their backs. She wore a pair of thin white knickers over her scrawny loins, doubtless specially selected for the occasion.

She started clambering into the netting which she seemed to have arranged into some sort of primitive frock.

'Won't you be cold?' asked Freddie prosaically.

He didn't want the Aylotts up in arms.

'Sacrifices have got to shiver and shake,' she said, 'it's part of the deal. Monsters just love jitters. A happy sacrifice doesn't taste so good. Tie me, chéri.'

Bertrand obliged with a piece of curtain tape that Isobel had thoughtfully provided for the occasion. She was soon

138

trussed up like a chicken to the stone. It did seem to lend itself to the activity, with just the right grooves and knobbly bits to put curtain tape round.

'Voilà,' said Bertrand.

'I'm practically dead with pleasure already, actually,' she said. 'I hope the monster doesn't take too long or I'll be gone.'

Freddie was beginning to have second thoughts about all this, but it was too late to pull out. Isobel was firmly in the driving seat.

'Now,' she said, when everything was to her satisfaction, 'all you guys have to do is wait around the corner. When the monster comes, I'll holler. Make sure you stand up to it, now.'

There seemed nothing for it but to retreat into the bushes and swig some more of Bertrand's brandy. As they went, Freddie turned for a last look at the sacrificial scene. He had to admit that, if he had happened to be a monster, he would have been moved.

Isobel, from a distance, in her white net, looked vulnerable and bait-like. She writhed a little when she saw him watching, and tried out a few piteous moans.

No monster could know, of course, what a little pill she was in reality. He dared say she'd give even a monster a severe bout of acid indigestion, but that was the monster's look-out.

The boys sat down on a tree stump near the water's edge, and began their vigil.

The brandy was passed back and forth several times, exerting a momentary cordial effect, but the breeze across the lake grew chill. Even the midges started to make for their oozy couches.

Sitting next to Bertrand, bottom to bottom, was all right, of course, but it merely served to stir up things that were better left unstirred up.

139

'We'd better go soon,' said Freddie. 'Old Aylott will give us the most frightful bollocking.'

Suddenly the air was rent by a scream.

'Yeeeow.'

It was Isobel sounding genuinely alarmed.

They dashed from their shelter and ran towards the rock. In the near-darkness, they saw a darker primal shape, goatman or troll, scuttling away across the clearing and disappearing into the bushes on the further side.

Of Isobel there was no trace.

'Oh fuck,' said Freddie. 'That's done it.'

'The monster make a good supper, I think,' said Bertrand.

'There is no monster,' said Freddie, angrily, 'it was a game.'

They spent some time searching around the clearing for any sign of the girl. But in the dark there was little hope of a clue. At least there seemed to be no blood.

A water bird of some kind started crying like a lost child across the lake.

'Oh fuck,' said Freddie again, 'this time we've done it. She's gone. They'll have to dredge the lake. God knows what Aylott's going to do. To say nothing of the police. It'll be in the newspapers. Girl tied to rock by teenage deviants. Foul play suspected.'

They trudged back glumly in the yellowing light of Freddie's pocket torch.

They paused outside Flat Foot while Freddie tried to think of the best way of putting it to the Aylotts.

'Could I just say we went for a walk and she must have taken a wrong turn in the dark? But what if they find her body with the white lace on? They'll know we're lying. Poor Isobel.'

Nerving himself for trouble, Freddie walked resolutely into Flat Foot's hall, determined to go and confess immediately. Then he stopped, imagining only too well the look of incredulity and rage on Mr Aylott's face.

'I'm afraid we've lost Isobel,' he could hear himself saying, 'that is, she disappeared.'

'Disappeared?'

'Yes, well, we sort of tied her to a rock, you see, like Andromeda.'

'Tied her to a rock? You what?'

Freddie had to admit, it sounded bad. In fact, it sounded worse than bad.

He started to walk away down the corridor towards their bedroom, and stopped again, familiar sensations of guilt and fear assailing him. Should one confess and face the punishment; or say nothing and hope to get away with it?

'We must quicken ourselves,' said Bertrand. 'The little pustule may be in danger.'

They knocked at the kitchen door, went in, found no sign of life and climbed the back stairs up to the Aylotts' quarters. In the corridor he paused again, Bertrand almost falling on top of him. Which door should they try? They crept along listening to each.

There were two silent rooms, and then, from the third, the sound of rhythmic bed-creaking and low animal noises. Freddie suddenly remembered what Isobel had said about the Aylotts trying to make a baby.

He couldn't go in, right in the middle of all that creaking; but, as Bertrand said, the thing was urgent. Isobel could be halfway to Hell's gate by now. He lifted his hand to rap at the door, imagining the consternation and sheet heaving that would ensue; and just as he did so, another door opened.

'Hi scumbag,' said the little pustule, indicating the creakers' door, 'I told you they'd be doing it.'

'Isobel,' the boys hissed.

'What the hell happened to you?' said Freddie.

'I got Jackie to untie me,' she said. 'He always watches out for me. I thought I'd give you creeps a scare. Fooled you, didn't I?'

'Aaaaagh,' said the Aylotts' door. 'Mmmmmfh.'

'They'll never make it,' said Isobel.

'Bitch,' said Freddie.

'Who can't take a joke, then?' said Isobel. 'By the way, did you see it?'

'See what?'

'The monster, of course, stupid.'

'There is no monster.'

'There is, you know.'

'You've fooled us once already.'

Isobel made enormous eyes at Bertrand.

'Well, you're a jerk if you don't believe me. It had a kind of snouty flat head, and more humps than the Aylotts have had tonight.'

'How many humps have the Aylotts had tonight?'

'Two.'

'So how many humps did the monster have?'

'Three. Now for Chrissakes can't a girl get some sleep around here?'

20

Next morning, Freddie woke with a slight headache.

He thought, if I'm going to have to spend another day looking at that lake, I'm going to derange myself. And then he remembered that today was the day of the tea-party at How Hall.

Encouraged, he even agreed to Bertrand's suggestion that they take a boat until lunchtime.

So, after breakfast, they formed up at the boatyard.

'Up and down, up and down,' said Jackie. 'I never knew such gluttons for punishment.'

They chose *Westminster Bridge*.

The mist that had been draping the lake was lifting like Freddie's headache, and a pale fuzzy brightish luminescence which passed for a good day in these parts was filtering through high cumulo-nimbus.

Bertrand pulled away to the headland beyond the place where they had stopped the day before. They traversed the lake three times, until the Hell Hall boathouse came into view. Freddie's watch was registering twelve o'clock, and he was just about to suggest that they start going back, when Bertrand gave a shout.

'Regarde, look, Freddie.'

Freddie turned, and his heart yo-yoed against his uvula. There, floating on the water, was a large reptilian fin. It seemed, against the odds, that Isobel had not been lying. It was evidently part of a monster.

'Is it alive?' faltered Freddie.

He did not wish to become part of a legend's lunch.

'Non, no. She does not move. She is flat. She is only a member.'

'But wh-where are the other members?' quavered Freddie.

A monster without its member might be a very angry monster indeed.

'Do you think we ought to go so close?'

'We must investigate.'

That damned French method scientific again.

Rowing on tiptoe, they approached the floating limb. It was about five feet long and, at its widest point, three feet broad. Would it be decomposing? Were there other organs bobbing below the surface?

Bertrand was busily sketching and making notes in his log. Very gingerly, he now reached out with an oar and poked the object. There was no stench, no scurry of bubbles.

Bertrand inserted the oar under the flipper and hoisted it aloft.

'Look out,' shouted Freddie in alarm, not wanting their trophy to disintegrate before the photographs were taken.

Bertrand merely hoicked the object in towards the boat, leant over, and held it up. Freddie saw that instead of slippery saurian it was a crudely stitched artefact of rubber and canvas.

'It is a drôlerie,' said Bertrand.

It was almost as if it had been put out as bait.

21

There was a shout from the shore.

'Hey, youth, come here.'

Mr Seathwaite had been watching their antics from the boathouse.

Freddie took up the oars while Bertrand trailed the limb through the water after them.

'We found a member,' said Freddie as they neared the quay.

'It's mine,' said Mr Seathwaite evenly. 'Damn thing fell off this morning. You'd better come ashore for lunch.'

It was their lunch Mr Seathwaite was thinking of. He wouldn't speak of the member until they'd had lunch, he said. He was mortified that there were no pork pies.

'Can't eat sandwiches,' he said. 'They make be gurk.'

However, he seemed to do pretty well on the luncheon meat and mustard.

There was also incredibly dry yellow cake, and fruit.

Bertrand's apple had a note stuck on it from Isobel: 'C'est une pomme d'amour, chéri.'

Mr Seathwaite didn't eat fruit but he read the note carefully.

'Who is this strumpet?' he asked.

Freddie described her.

'Look out, youth,' Mr Seathwaite advised Bertrand. 'She'll have the breeches off you.'

'She's only thirteen,' said Freddie.

'They are remorseless,' said Mr Seathwaite. 'All men are boys at heart, and all little girls are women.'

'What about the flipper?' asked Freddie, as Mr Seathwaite, sated, addressed himself to a mug of whisky.

'Ah yes, the flipper. Well, now. I wonder if I should tell you. Can you keep a secret, youth?'

'I believe so,' said Freddie, 'and Bertrand can because his uncle was in the Resistance.'

'Well, then,' said Mr Seathwaite, 'if you promise not to tell a soul, or I shall come after you with instruments of the most exquisite torment, I am mending the family monster.'

People didn't say things like that in Bedfordshire.

'W . . . why?' asked Freddie.

'Why? The youth asks why! Did youths ask Dr Frankenstein why when he made his creature? No, they did not. They were properly awed and appalled. But since you ask, I will tell you. Your mention of monsters the other day put me in mind of it. I am mending it for what we call the Ettenwater Regatta. It will create something of a stir.'

'You mean, it's a hoax?' asked Freddie.

'You could call it that,' said Mr Seathwaite. 'I prefer to call it the apotheosis of a myth. The monster was designed and made under the direction of my Great-Uncle Gussie. Gussie was something of a scientist as well as a practical joker – it was a time, you know, of great hoaxes. Poor old Uncle Gussie . . . the Huns got him in 1917 before he could make the thing famous.'

'Why did he do it?'

'Why does one perpetrate a hoax? You know what Ettenwater means, youth?'

'Well . . .'

'It means giant water, troll water, ogre water or, if you like, monster water. The Saxon word "etain" has all those meanings.'

'I read something about it in a book at the guesthouse.'

'They were always superstitious about the lake in these

146

parts. As you see, there are few farm buildings. There is not much land, of course, to farm. It is a hard land, youth. My family has lived round here, growing poorer and poorer, for centuries. Mad buggers to come here in the first place. Uncle Gussie wanted to cock a snook at all that. Look where it got him. Still, I think it would add cheer to the Regatta, don't you?'

'Absolutely, rather,' said Freddie, and then: 'Is it true the lake's haunted?'

'It is more than haunted. Oh, there are ghosts. The monk who rescued fallen women, and then fell in love with one and killed himself, silly bugger. His spirit cries up in the quarry over Muckle Pass.'

He pointed up the hillside to where the boys had walked yesterday. It was true; there had been a peculiar melancholy about the place.

'Some swear the lake is bottomless,' continued Mr Seathwaite. 'They used to say it led straight down to Hell. L'enfer,' he added for Bertrand's benefit, pointing to the ground.

'Bien sûr,' said Bertrand, as though the location of one of Hell's doors was an everyday affair.

'Certainly there have been drownings where the bodies have never been recovered,' said Mr Seathwaite, pulling out and lighting a hellish-smelling pipe. 'There were some frogmen doing tests on new equipment. One of them never came up. But the guesthouse proprietor who murdered his wife here just before the war, rolled her up in a carpet and weighed her down with stones, he was unlucky. She bobbed up to the surface with her eyes eaten out by the fish.'

'Ugh,' said Freddie.

'Yes, it was rather. Funny thing was they almost didn't get the husband. They couldn't identify her by her teeth. Someone . . . or something . . . had taken all her gold fillings out. You will observe that Great-Uncle Gussie had much credulity to draw upon.'

'We thought we saw something on the lakes – a sort of swirly ripply sort of thing,' said Freddie.

'Underwater current,' said Mr Seathwaite. 'Lots of those. There are no monsters any more. Otherwise we should not need to invent them.'

'Oh,' said Freddie, thinking of the wasted muscle power. Then he thought of something else.

'Do you know anything about somebody with the initials J.S. and what happened in August 1940?'

Mr Seathwaite's brow clouded.

'What . . . who told you that, youth?'

'We saw it on a stone. I didn't know it was important.'

Mr Seathwaite heaved a great sigh. He seemed to go into a decline.

'Could we see the monster?' asked Freddie at last.

'What? Oh. Yes . . . yes, if you have to . . .'

He led them to the far side of the boathouse where, neatly stowed, were what looked like yards of slimy-looking dark green canvas.

Mr Seathwaite regained his jauntier manner as they inspected it.

'We sometimes used to try and work it as children, but even then it was sadly neglected. However, I have the old boy's plans to work on, and I've included some modifications of my own. It is modelled on the plesiosaur but it is a somewhat free interpretation. The head I keep else-where,' he told them, 'far from prying eyes. My repairs are nearly complete. I insert rubber tubing derived from aircraft inner tubes, and welded by a man I know. I inflate. I experiment with ballast. And then, this is the masterstroke, take out the air but insert decaying matter of some kind into the rubber.'

'Decaying matter?' repeated Freddie.

The man really was mad.

'A rabbit or two, a cat, a squirrel, perhaps even a lamb, or for the squeamish, rotting vegetation. We seal the rubber and let nature do the rest. The anaerobic microbes fill the rubber with gas, the monster rises to the surface, the pressure valve expels the gas, the monster sinks. And the process begins again. Ingenious, is it not?'

'How do you know when the monster will rise to the surface?'

'My calculations are that it will surface exactly forty-three hours, twenty minutes after submerging. I have been doing considerable experimentation and Uncle Gussie's notes are exhaustive. The Regatta's firework display starts at eight o'clock, just when the light is fading. That is the optimum moment for a manifestation. Everyone will be watching, and the dusk will conceal the imperfections of my stitching. I am concentrating on effect, not detail . . . What do you say, youth? I shall require assistance.'

Freddie had the sensation of bait being laid again.

'Well,' he said, looking at Bertrand who gave his famous shrug, 'I don't know, I suppose so, yes. It's better than rowing up and down in the rain. But are you sure it's . . . all right?'

'All right? Ha!' Mr Seathwaite rolled his eyes. 'What a youth! It's a lot more all right than what passes for all right these days. All right, he asks. Foh! Giving innocent pleasure to the groundlings? What could be more all right than that?'

'The other thing is,' said Freddie, 'we're going up for tea. Can we leave our boat here and collect it on the way back? There's no time to take it back now.'

'You're going up there? What d'you want to go up there for? I can't imagine why anyone should want to go up there. You'd far better stay down here, you know. We

149

could go for a trip in *Proserpine*. There is more for you to see.'

'We're going to tea,' said Freddie. 'Cream cakes and things. We haven't had a decent meal for days.'

'Well, don't bloody say anything. Mum's the word.'

'Honour,' said Freddie. 'Absolutely scout's.'

'Going to tea,' reiterated Mr Seathwaite, 'going to tea up there? Ha! Mind there's no ground glass in it.'

Freddie thought of something.

'Did you by any chance collect scraps of food from How Rock?'

'Indeed I did. Most fortuitous. I took it as a portent. Did you leave it there?'

'Yes.'

'Strange youth. Bring it straight round here next time. The maw gapes.'

Outside, the cloud had thickened and now precipitated in a shower.

22

They walked up in the rain to the big house, pondering these matters. Mrs Seathwaite was there to greet them before they even had time to ring the doorbell.

'Awful weather,' she said. 'You must be wet through.'

'It's all right,' said Freddie. 'We only had to come up from the boathouse.'

Her handsome face darkened.

'I say,' she said. 'Do you have to go there? I'd give it a wide berth if I were you.'

'Oh,' said Freddie. 'Sorry.'

'Anyway, come in and have a chocolate. What time do you have your evening meal?'

'We have high tea at six,' said Freddie. 'It's pretty horrible.'

'We'll have our tea at four,' she said. 'That'll give us time to work up an appetite. Now . . . what would you like to do? If only it was fine we could play tennis, but there are puddles all over the court. Ping-pong?'

Bertrand was about to say yes, but Freddie didn't want to spoil the afternoon by feeling bad-tempered about losing.

'Couldn't I play the piano?' he asked.

He had been itching to get his hands on the Bechstein.

'Absolutely,' said Mrs Seathwaite. 'Go right ahead. Play like billy-oh. You'll find some music – I think there's a hymnbook – in the piano-stool. But we know you don't like an audience, so I'll take Bertrand round the garden.'

'D'accord.'

'Sure you'll be all right, Freddie?'

'I'll be fine,' said Freddie, though he was beginning to feel he'd made a mistake.

There was something about the way she took Bertrand's hand that he didn't like again. He watched them go out through the French windows with a lover's sense of impermanence. It suddenly struck him that he only had nine more days before he and Bertrand went back to Bedfordshire, and Bertrand returned from there to France. Why had he been such a fool about the ping-pong? Couldn't he even bear to be beaten by his best-beloved?

Stifling his apprehensions, he addressed himself to the hymnbook (it was a green-backed English Hymnal, his favourite). The very first page he opened was a winner. 'Immortal, Invisible' (even though it had four flats), and he knew that nearby would be Jeremiah Clarke's setting of J. G. Whittier's 'Immortal Love for ever full', which seemed particularly appropriate at the moment. From here, having played all five verses, he flipped to 'O worship the King', and 'Rejoice, the Lord is King' by Handel, and 'Rejoice, O Land, in God thy might' by W. Knapp, rejoicing in the clear bright tones of the Bechstein and the perfect precision of its milky-white keys.

Then he turned to Evening, and played 'Abide with me' and Bishop Ken's 'Glory to Thee, my God, this night' in the ordinary and, triumphantly, the descant version.

The Bechstein seemed so to improve his playing that he found the hymns for once unsatisfying, and he opened the piano-stool and delved inside for the promised books. He was confronted by the most wonderful selection of playable music – Easy Classics of Bach, Handel, Mozart, Haydn, Beethoven – The Daily Express Community Song Book – Strauss Waltzes – Simple Songs from the Opera – Baroque Masterworks – The World's Top Twenty Piano

Solos. There was matter here for a month of wet afternoons.

Strange that it should all be here, so new-looking, as if it were waiting for him.

He became unaware of time, as he had been on so many days at home, when the minutes scurried past like the cascading demi-semiquavers in the last Variation of the Harmonious Blacksmith, though rather more smoothly executed.

Glancing out of the window at one point, he thought he saw Mrs Seathwaite and Bertrand running along a distant alley near a little witch's hut summerhouse, but it could have been the wind swinging the nervous sunlight between the branches of the cedar and casting skittish shadows on the grass.

Finally, however, he paused. He looked at the clock on the chimneypiece. It was twenty past four. He was incredulous that the hour should be so late.

A strange apprehension mingled with annoyance seized him. Had something happened to them? If they left it any longer they'd be too late to have the famous tea anyway. Should he go and look for them? Where should he start?

He opened the door into the hall. A delicious smell of toast was coming from somewhere. He followed it until he found Mrs Seathwaite and Bertrand standing at the Aga making anchovy soldiers.

'There he is,' she said. 'We didn't like to disturb you. You were playing like Paderewski.'

It wasn't true, but Freddie was slightly mollified.

Sitting in the drawing room gorging himself on the cakes from Ambleside which certainly had not been overpraised, he felt relaxed enough to ask what he afterwards realized was a stupid question.

'Doesn't Mr Seathwaite have tea?'

He knew at once that he had made a mistake. She

stopped in mid-laugh at something Bertrand had said, and the brow darkened again.

'Mr Seathwaite does not take tea. I very much doubt whether Mr Seathwaite takes anything at all except . . . I say, let's not talk about Mr Seathwaite. Ever read Henry Fielding, Freddie? Remember where he talks about "that monstrous animal, a husband and wife"? I daresay you will learn all about it sometime. Meanwhile, we are jolly enough as we are. More cake? Encore de gâteau?'

But it was already late. A cloud had gathered over the occasion. They said a hasty goodbye to Mrs Seathwaite.

'You must come round again soon. Day after tomorrow?'

'Jolly good,' said Bertrand who seemed to be catching on fast.

'Goodbye. Toodle-bung.'

They ran down to the boathouse where Mr Seathwaite in dirty blazer, yellowed trousers and nautical cap, was at the helm of *Proserpine*, steam up, with *Westminster Bridge* nodding on a painter at the stern. In honour of the occasion, even the weather was improving.

'How was tea?' enquired Mr Seathwaite. 'Don't puke on *Proserpine*.'

He gave them a brief disquisition on the steamboat which they'd both been itching to board all through the cream cakes.

Much of *Proserpine*'s space had originally been taken up by the steam engine itself, he said. She had been coal-fired, and there had been little room for anything but coal – but she had been converted to burn oil years ago, and the cabin had been built aft.

Freddie peered inside. There was a small screen on a table together with a couple of large knobby instruments that looked like overgrown wirelesses. He thought he recognized one of them from Mr Seathwaite's den.

'Now,' said Mr Seathwaite, 'before I take you back, this is what we're going to do. Pull out the chart from that locker, youth.'

Freddie extricated a large-scale map of the lake and fitted as much as he could upon the table.

'At this end,' said Mr Seathwaite, pointing a black fingernail, 'the water is some 350 foot deep, possibly more. I have already this year traversed half the area – see, I've marked it in red. We will now traverse from point L to point M, and then crisscross in classically recommended manner.'

'Recommended by whom?' asked Freddie.

'By the school of submarine warfare of course. You ask the most primitive questions, youth.'

'Were you in submarines?'

'Well, er no, not exactly.'

'What were you in?' persisted Freddie.

'I was in reserve, youth. They wouldn't let me fight. I was an inventor. I did some Admiralty work. And farming, of course.'

'My father was in the Navy,' said Freddie. 'He was killed when the *Hood* blew up.'

'Bad show,' said Mr Seathwaite.

He seemed momentarily plunged in gloom.

'It was all over very quickly,' said Freddie, alleviatingly, 'they said he couldn't have suffered. I hardly knew him really.'

'Got any of that cake still?' asked Mr Seathwaite.

'I think there's a piece left.'

'Might be better with a drop of whisky.'

Mr Seathwaite poured a generous dollop from his glass over the saffron slab, popped a piece in his mouth and nodded vigorously.

'Much better,' he said, gurking.

Freddie and Bertrand looked at each other. They were impatient to be off.

'You told her you were coming out with me, youth?' said Mr Seathwaite, gesturing up at the house. 'Shouldn't have done that. Hell Hall hath no fury like Mrs Seathwaite scorned.'

'I'm sorry,' said Freddie.

'Can't be helped . . . youth. I wouldn't tell her anything if I were you. Mum's the word. Careless talk and so forth.'

'Sorry,' said Freddie again. 'But we didn't scorn her. It surely doesn't matter between friends?'

'Mrs Seathwaite is no friend of mine. That woman can find scorn in a teacup.'

'Oh,' said Freddie.

'Come and look at the engine room,' said Mr Seathwaite, mopping the last crumbs with his forefinger and putting the resulting squidge in his mouth.

The engine was a glorious work, a little brass and copper monster flanked by dials. Steam was already beginning to drift from a valve, its wisp intent on catching the cloudlet from the funnel and always just failing as they slid under the water gate.

If Mr Seathwaite had deliberately set out to counter the blandishments of his wife, there was no doubt he was countering splendidly.

'There's the water tank. We pick it up when it gets low, automatically. Useful that. On some of these you have to do it by hand. If you forget, you could end up feeding the seagulls. That's the safety valve. Don't touch the boiler. Hot as hell.'

There was a small brass plaque on the boiler which said Phipps & Cardale, Broughton-in-Furness 1894, and a little dark-glass peephole in a hinged door through which Freddie could see the glint of fire winking like mischief in a pig's eye. The dial marked PRESSURE PSI was reading 22.

'When it's up to forty,' said Mr Seathwaite, 'we'll be ready to go.'

'What happens when it gets to one twenty?' asked Freddie, noting the red at the end of the dial.

'It explodes,' said Mr Seathwaite.

'What vitesse?' asked Bertrand who had been, though silent, keenly attentive.

'Oh, about six knots in a following wind,' said Mr Seathwaite. 'Translate, would you, youth. It's almost seven and a half miles an hour.'

'C'est à dire, douze kilomètres par heure dans un vent suivant,' Freddie explained, rather well, he thought.

'Formidable.'

Freddie hadn't seen Bertrand so worked up about anything, not even the monster, not even Mrs Seathwaite. He stroked the air lovingly about the rounded belly of the metal, making Freddie wish that he too had been built in Broughton-in-Furness in 1894.

'It is permitted to drive him?' asked Bertrand.

'When we're out on the lake, he can drive him a bit if he likes,' said Mr Seathwaite, 'but he must bloody well do as I tell him or we'll be up shit creek. Come inside, youth, and I'll show you how the echo-sounder works. It is my own invention or shall I say adaptation. Several parties are interested.'

He took Freddie back into the cabin, and turned one of the knobs on the equipment. A light came on and a blip-blip-blipping noise started to sound.

'That is the bottom of the boathouse we are hearing, youth. When we are out in deeper water, you will only hear that sound if something large is underneath us. This is the scanner.'

157

He turned another knob, and the screen lit up. Freddie's acquaintance with *The Cruel Sea* gave him a certain familiarity with the principles of the device. Mr Seathwaite showed him how to read the screen for distance and direction.

'If you see a little solid fuzz becoming clearer, shout like hell. It'll probably be a log. But tell me where it is, port or starboard. I need to follow it. You realize this is a dubious undertaking, don't you, youth?'

'Yes,' said Freddie.

'Good. It is best to start such quests from a scientific standpoint.'

The wind had been dropping while they had tea, and now the sky for the first time in a week showed palpable signs of blue. The boys opened the boathouse doors, cast off, and the *Proserpine* edged out into the lake blowing smoke and steam in ragged buntings as she gathered way.

'Tell me when the echo-sounder's lost the bottom, youth,' said Mr Seathwaite.

Freddie scanned the screen attentively, bottling up the questions he wanted to ask. Blip . . . blip . . . blipblip . . .

'Now,' yelled Freddie.

Bertrand took the wheel, and Mr Seathwaite sat in his captain's chair, smoking a pipe and surveying the surroundings with gloomy satisfaction.

They moved up and down across the lake for perhaps half an hour while the sun shone upon them, and the propeller chewed at the water in soothing susurrations.

'Watch that screen, youth.'

'Sorry.'

The lake seemed so innocent this afternoon that, as the wavelets scampered past, Freddie wondered whether Mr Seathwaite had been having him on about the corpses and the teeth; but the man looked so rapt, his veiny bright eyes were so intent, that Freddie felt he at least believed

158

it to be true. He was debating whether to question him further when he was distracted by a noise from the machine.

Blip blip blipblipblip.

He glanced quickly at the screen. Was there something there? Yes, a little fuzzy iota off to the right.

'Quick, where is it, youth?

'Er . . . starboard,' said Freddie.

Mr Seathwaite seized the wheel, and *Proserpine* swung round. Even as she did so, the sound faded and the iota vanished.

'Sorry,' said Freddie.

'Not your fault, youth, probably a log. Even so, we'll mark it on the chart.'

He entered the cabin and showed Freddie where to put the cross, some three inches from the last mark.

'There's just one thing,' said Freddie; something had been bothering him.

'Yes, youth.'

'What exactly are we looking for? Not a monster, I take it.'

'Just testing,' said Mr Seathwaite. 'If I get this thing right, I can start talking to the Fisheries people, might even make some cash. Thing is, I put a weighted target down and I can't find the bugger. I am out in all weathers. Nobody can say I haven't tried.'

He didn't seem inclined to talk about it further, so Freddie let the matter drop. Mr Seathwaite seemed to have taken on the mantle of Flying Dutchman as well as St Sebastian. It was extraordinary how the extraordinary seemed to be the norm up here.

'Is that why you call your house Hell Hall?' he asked.

Mr Seathwaite's brow darkened.

'Is what why, youth?'

'Because of the gates to Hell being under the lake?'

159

'No,' said Mr Seathwaite, 'that is incidental. Hell has many avenues.'

And he would say no more on that subject either.

'I suppose,' said Freddie, 'you could locate one of the missing dead bodies with this machine.'

'You can suppose what you like, youth.'

They continued their traverse of the lake in silence, the sonar mute as its deviser.

Freddie was beginning to doubt that any further conversation was to be had from him that day – or quite possibly on any other occasion – when a flash of colour along the shore roused him from his moody reverie.

'See that, youth?'

'What is it?'

'That is a halcyon, a kingfisher. Don't usually have 'em round here.'

'Is it good luck?'

'I shouldn't think so.'

'Oh.'

'Why should it be good luck?'

'I don't know.'

'Do you need good luck, youth?'

'Yes, well, probably.'

'Do you have bad luck?'

'Well, sometimes.'

He was going to say that this whole holiday had seemed like bad luck but thought it might be mannerless to his host as well as disloyal to his mother.

'You don't know what bad luck is, youth.'

'No, well, I suppose I don't.'

'You come here – on board my boat – and talk about bad luck. Get off.'

'What?'

'Go on. You hear me. Get off my boat.'

Mr Seathwaite was looming over him now, flushed and

menacing. Bertrand looked round curiously, hearing the raised voices above the chuntering of the engine.

'I can't,' said Freddie. 'It's the middle of the lake.'

'It's the middle of the lake,' mimicked Mr Seathwaite. 'Youth doesn't want to get his clothes wet. You can have no idea what bad luck is, youth. Jump.'

He grabbed Freddie and pushed him up against the rail.

'Jump.'

'No.'

'Go on, jump, you snivelling little tosser.'

'No, I . . .'

Freddie was trying desperately not to cry but he was helped by the certainty that if he did so it would give Mr Seathwaite enormous satisfaction. As the shoreline approached at the end of their traverse, he was actually about to throw himself into the water rather than argue the point, when Mr Seathwaite caught him by the collar.

'Just testing you, youth.'

'Qu'est-ce qui arrive?' shouted Bertrand, leaving the helm and moving up to them.

Proserpine was now running straight for the shore.

Freddie pointed, horrified, at the approaching shallows. Mr Seathwaite laughed. Bertrand stood there like a distracted lemming. Freddie rushed up to the wheel and threw the vessel round. He could see the rocks streaming away below him. The man was clearly deranged.

PIP PIP PIPIP, sang the sonar.

'Hard a-port,' shouted Mr Seathwaite.

PIPIPIPIPIP . . . pipip . . . pip . . .

'There's something in this fucking lake,' said Mr Seathwaite. 'Sound the siren, youth.'

Freddie tugged the lanyard, and a great doleful cry echoed across the water. It was the sound the boys had heard on their first evening.

'Deep calling unto deep,' said Mr Seathwaite.

There was no knowing, of course, thought Freddie, whether the echo-sounder really worked at all, or whether it just made noises now and then. He didn't voice the speculation.

Mr Seathwaite put the engine into neutral, and they crowded the rail, peering at the water. Nothing stirred. Not a flicker of a corpse, not a snubbing of a snout, not even a weighty target disturbed the depths. Only the reflections of their faces, corrugated in the lapping brown translucence of the water, winked back at them.

'Well done, youths,' said Mr Seathwaite. 'Back to base. You must return for your tea, and I have much to do before our monster can face his public.'

23

When they finally reached Flat Foot, having astonished Jackie by arriving in style on *Proserpine* with *Westminster Bridge* dancing in her wake, they found they had cut it rather fine again. It was just three minutes to six.

Entering, they found Mrs Aylott talking on the telephone in the hall. She motioned to Freddie.

'Here he is,' she said to the telephone, 'oh no, no trouble,' and then to Freddie: 'It's your mother.'

'Hullo, Mum,' he said, taking the telephone.

Bertrand stood beside him, doing his dobbin act, making Freddie ashamed of the feelings which would so much hurt Mother. No one was a homo in the family, it was the most awful blight. And yet, he couldn't put any other interpretation on what he felt for the French boy. It was a feeling beyond mere schoolish little-boy girl substitutes. It was absurd that it should so come to him now, just when he should be feeling all normal and filial.

Everything was well at Castle Coupar, Mother informed him. She hadn't rung before because she'd wanted them to settle down, and Mrs Aylott said they'd settled down very nicely. She was so glad. She'd known they would enjoy themselves. She and Rollo had arrived at the Castle just in time for a drink before dinner. It was just as well the boys hadn't come because the castle, big though it was, was full of cousins, and they'd already had a couple of rather grand dinner parties which would have bored the boys to bits. How was Bertrand?

'Bertrand's all right. He's fine.'

'And Flat Foot? How are you getting on with the goat's

163

milk? Would you like me to talk to Mrs Aylott about finding you some ordinary milk?'

'No, no. It's all right.'

'And the weather? We've had quite a lot of sun up here. Have you had sun?'

'The weather's all right.'

'Well, that's good. Everything's all right, then. I thought it wouldn't be so bad once you'd settled down. Have you been to see the Seathwaites?'

'Yes. We went to tea today.'

'Oh good. What are they like?'

'They're all right.'

'Well, that's nice. Her mother was such a friend of Cousin Percy's. There was that funny story about them. I'm trying to remember . . . no, it's gone.'

Freddie felt he should throw in some local colour. His mother might have been talking from Mars.

'Mr Seathwaite took us on his boat. It's a steamer.'

'He has a steamer?'

'Only a little one. He's got a mon . . .'

Freddie was going to tell her about the monster, and then he remembered Mr Seathwaite's insistence on secrecy, so he stopped.

'He's got a mon?' asked his mother, puzzled.

'He's er . . .' Freddie searched for inspiration, 'he's got a monk. A ghost that's supposed to cry. It's a local legend.'

He was rather good at lying.

'Well, that's nice,' said his mother.

Luckily, her mind was so full of thoughts that often she simply didn't register what you were saying.

'And Bertrand's enjoying himself?'

'He seems fine.'

'I'm so glad. I spoke to his mother and she says his sister's having a nice time with the Weatherbys too.'

'Would you like to talk to him?'

'Oh yes.'

He handed the telephone to Bertrand. He could hear his mother chirping away.

'Oui. Oui. Oui. Si. We are having a nice time. Goodbye,' said Bertrand, handing the telephone back to Freddie.

'Oh dear, there's the first dinner gong going,' said his mother, 'I'd better go and change. Look after yourselves. We'll see you next week. I'll ring you up to let you know what time. Goodbye, darling. Oh, hang on. Rollo wants a word.'

'Goodbye, Mum,' said Freddie.

'Is that Frap?'

'Yes.'

He could hear the first drink of the evening in Rollo's voice.

'Getting plenty of goat's milk, Frap? And do they give you goat's butter too?'

'No,' said Freddie evenly, 'they don't do butter.'

'Oh, bad luck, Frap,' said Rollo. 'Hard goat's cheeeeese.'

24

Freddie woke to the routine percussion of rain-laden wind rattling and spattering the window. The chilly sound coincided with the little shiver in his stomach as he looked across at the bed where Bertrand lay sleeping. He now knew himself to be in love with Bertrand.

It was ridiculous, of course. Bertrand had disclosed so little of himself – whether because of language, culture or personality – who knew? But any notion of the marriage of true minds had to be ruled out.

Perhaps it was the very absence of real knowledge that made him feel like this, thought Freddie. When everything was guessable, anything was possible.

At all events, he recognized the bittersweet, half painful, half exhilarating sensations that he had first experienced at the age of five when he had loved a girl called Bridget who did wondrous handstands on the beach and could play real tunes on her recorder – not, it had to be said, at the same time. His sensibilities had been so stirred that he had wet his bed – a thing he had not done for many months – while staying in her house.

Later, the same sensations, if not the night pissing, had been evoked at his first boarding school when he had entered upon a close affinity with another boy called Flamsteed. It had become so puzzlingly intense that he had had to end it. He had shared a desk with another boy at the beginning of the following term – it was his first great betrayal.

This had been followed, three or four years later, by a passion for a girl, daughter of some friends of his parents, who had come to stay in the holidays when he was nearly fourteen. They had held hands and kissed, and her little breasts had ached, and his withers had been wrung, and when the time of parting came, he promised to write to her at school.

The delicious sadness, the stone in the stomach, had been somewhat eased by writing the letter in the first week of term. It was a well-turned effort, drawing from his readings of the short stories of Sapper and the Golden Treasury, and he was rather pleased with it. But there was no reply.

He paused, then wrote again in more passionate tones; and while May wore on, and the smell of new paint in the dorm subsided to be overtaken by the fragance of fresh-cut grass, he waited for an answer.

He wrote a third and a fourth, but nothing was forth-coming. He was beginning to lose interest now, especcially because he had just been awarded his First Eleven Colours, and it was more pique than passion that prompted him to write a fifth.

Perhaps because it did not come from the heart, he poured into it everything he knew, and much that he didn't. He praised her eyes, her beauteous form, her kisses which burned him like the fire which never dies, he yearned to be in her arms again, spinning in a vortex of heedless rapture.

He checked the address: Convent of the Holy Child, Leeming-on-Crouch; and sent it off in a clean blue envelope.

This time he did get a reply. It arrived within a week. He carried it round all morning until he could open it alone in the lav. His fingers trembled. His passion was miraculously revived. At last he allowed himself to read her rounded schoolgirl hand.

The letter was short and to the point.

'Dear Freddie,' it read, 'Please do not write me any more letters because all our letters are opened by one of the Sisters, and read out to the whole school. Yours, Teresa.'

He was so embarrassed, he wanted to disappear down the lavatory seat and pull the chain. Why had she asked him to write to her at all? He did not understand women.

But he did, he thought, understand true love as he feasted his eyes on the dormant Bertrand.

Lines from 'Lead Kindly Light', to the tune of Lux Benigna, came to his mind:

> 'And with the morn those angel faces smile,
> Which I have loved long since, and lost awhile . . .'

Was this, then, really it?

Being a true homosexual, someone who really preferred men (rather than playing around with boys merely as girl-substitutes), was one of the great fears expressed by middle-school men in late-night conversations in the House bathroom. It was like wondering whether you were going to need glasses or get polio.

Boys like the aptly named Stickly-Manning, who was as queer as a coot, didn't mind in the least being a homo, but most people had the conventional horror of being different. Anyway, you could be put in prison for that kind of thing, and your people would be dreadfully upset.

He got out of bed and went to the wash-basin, splashing his face with cold water as if to cleanse himself of oddity.

He needed a shave. While he performed this twice a week ritual, he noticed Bertrand watching him from his bed. Bertrand never seemed to need one.

To deflect the boy's attention from the monster that was slowly climbing up his pyjamas, he flicked some water at him.

168

'Come on, paresseux, time to get up.'

Bertrand rose and dressed with even more than his usual shyness. Did he after all realize Freddie's passion?

In the dining room, there was no Isobel this morning. Mrs Aylott said she'd caught the bus into Whitehaven with Mr Aylott, who had to see to some business. She was going to the dentist about her plate.

Mrs Aylott handed them their boiled eggs and the teapot in her usual question and answer manner.

'There you are then, is that all right for you? Good.'

Later, Freddie went into the kitchen to ask for the toast, and found Mrs Aylott crying into the washing-up bowl.

She straightened up and wiped her eyes and pretended she'd been peeling onions, but you could always tell when someone was blubbing for real.

Freddie smiled at her hopelessly, wanting to help, but the grief of grownups always made him nervous.

'We've had to sell up,' she said at last, 'we just can't make ends meet here. They're paying good money. It'll be like a Holiday Hamlet next year if they get permission. Mr Leacock introduced them, they were the couple who stayed here and saw a monster, or said they did. You'll be the last people we'll be having here.'

'I'm sorry,' said Freddie. 'Is there anything I can do?'

'You're a good lad,' smiled Mrs Aylott through her tears. 'But there's nothing anyone can do.'

The telephone rang. It was Mrs Seathwaite calling them to lunch.

25

There was chicken and roast potatoes and bread sauce, followed by raspberries and cream.

Bertrand could hardly believe that England could furnish such delights. He became quite dreamy with gastronomic lust.

After lunch, Mrs Seathwaite assumed Freddie would want to play the piano again – an assumption she made, Freddie thought, a little too readily. In point of fact, he would rather have trailed round the garden with her and Bertrand, but it was becoming clear to him that Mrs Seathwaite had cast herself in the Bertrand-hogging role.

In fact, he had to say it, it looked as if she was flirting with him. Could it be possible? He recalled what Aitken had said in the House bathroom one night.

'Older women,' said Aitken, adjusting his big pink buttocks on the wash-basins, 'older women cream their knickers for men of our age. They just can't get enough of us. You see, we're at our sexual peak. Once a man's over twenty, it's just one long fall-off. Make hay while the bums shine, that's what I say.'

Was this what lay behind Mrs Seathwaite's unfathomable spectacles? Were her loins really in turmoil under her neatly pleated blue skirt?

Freddie sat down obediently at the piano and played everything in the piano-stool. There seemed to be even more music books than on the day before. She must have been loading them up, to make quite sure he wouldn't disturb her and Bertrand at whatever it was they were doing. He was sure he had heard them go upstairs. They

170

were probably in the bed going at it hammer and tongs while he sat down here playing the Harmonious Blacksmith like a donkey.

He could not move from the piano – that would have been admitting jealousy. He had to sit and play while they played the beast with two backs. He couldn't take much more of this. He was going to have to run from the house, he wasn't going to come here again. Images of the utmost indecency filled his brain – the two of them writhing like earthworms on silken sheets – while the ordered measures of hymn and Handel dripped from his fingers.

At last Mrs Seathwaite and Bertrand returned.

'That was so nice, Freddie,' she said. 'You play like Millicent Silver. It's such a pity my nieces aren't here,' she went on.

'Do they like music?' asked Freddie.

'Well, not exactly. They're rather horsy on the whole. They'd probably like it if you played Light Cavalry. But what I really meant was, they'd entertain you so much better than I can. You must come over for a ride as soon as they are back. Bertrand tells me he doesn't, but I'm sure you'd like to. You could go out all day.'

'That'd be wonderful,' said Freddie, politely, though he didn't much care for horses.

He could never understand why such large animals could be stupid enough to let people ride them.

'Horses have souls, you know,' said Mrs Seathwaite. 'I believe we've all been here before. It's extraordinary but I feel Bertrand and I have already met. You, Freddie, are more of a stranger.'

'Thank you so much for tea,' said Freddie, slightly nettled, 'but I think Bertrand and I should be getting back now.'

'Of course. Goodbye. Goodbye, Bertrand. Come again soon.'

'Goodbye, Madame Seathwaite.'

'Au revoir.'

'Goodbye.'

Isobel was waiting for them when they got back. She had a red mark on her cheek and seemed to have been crying.

'What's up?' asked Freddie.

It was crying day for everyone.

'You've got to help me run away,' she said.

'Why?'

'She hit me.'

Mrs Aylott seemed such an unlikely candidate for violence that Freddie looked sceptical.

'It's true.'

'But why?'

'She said I was making eyes at Jackie down the lake.'

'And were you?'

'Course not. He's the only one for me.'

She smiled at Bertrand, who looked away.

'Don't you think you're a bit young for all this?' asked Freddie.

'I'm nearly fourteen,' she said. 'If you're big enough, you're old enough.'

It had all been said before, but there was sometimes a ritual quality about conversations with Isobel.

'But you're not big enough,' he objected.

'How do you know?' she said. 'Anyway I'm sorry for old Jackie. He's not got a girlfriend. And another thing, who's talking? You think about it all the time.'

'I'm not going to argue about it,' said Freddie, suddenly feeling sorry for the lonely giant, 'but I'd leave Jackie alone if I were you.'

'It's only fun, can't I have a bit of fun in this dump? They just louse me up because they can't have a kid of their own.'

'Back to work,' said Mrs Aylott, appearing in her kitchen apron, 'work'll keep you out of trouble, my girl. Hullo, boys. Just in time for tea. Pilchards on toast. I got them in special, like.'

In due course, the promised fish appeared, swathed in acrid tomato sauce, and sitting uneasily on top of lunch's cream. Bertrand chewed away with a look on his face that indicated taste buds turned down to zero. The boy seemed anyway to be preoccupied. Freddie tried to enthuse him, with a lover's zeal, with talk of the planned trip to Mr Seathwaite for the monster's trials, but Bertrand wouldn't be drawn. Indeed he surprised Freddie by finally shaking his head.

'I not come,' he said.

'Not come?' expostulated Freddie. 'Of course you're coming.'

'I not come,' the boy repeated mulishly. 'I am feeling terminated.'

Freddie became angry. There was an odd atmosphere in the place this evening, and it wasn't just the pilchards. What on earth had got into everybody?

'I suppose you want to fool around with that little tart,' he blurted suddenly, his frustration injudiciously manifesting It was an absurd line of argument. Isobel was more like a rather irritating younger sister than a prick teaser.

'Tarte? I do not like to eat a tart now after the mauvais poisson.'

The boy knew perfectly well what he meant.

'Cocotte,' said Freddie, finding the mot juste. 'Isobel la Cocotte. You want to play with her?'

'Bien sûr,' said Bertrand, entering into the spirit of the fracas.

'She's too young,' shouted Freddie. 'She's only thirteen.'

'She is charmante,' said Bertrand. 'Tomorrow I play wiz her.'

Bertrand said he had a migraine after tea, and wanted to go and lie down, so Freddie took himself off to the Res Lounge where he coaxed Lita Roza out of Daventry singing 'Slow Boat to China', and dipped once more into *Roving Through Lakeland*. But he was restless. He stood up, paced the room, walked out into the hall towards the front door. He had grown so used to the notion of bad weather that he now automatically assumed that if the light were low it would be raining, but the evening was clear, and only gentle breezes were blowing off the western hills. A pearly light suffused both lake and sky. Mr Seathwaite's reveille sounded mournfully across the water.

He walked down to the lakeside. The scene provided balm for his fever. Midges, sporting on the surface, reminded him of the pointless haphazard skitterings of human life (*The Rubaiyat of Omar Khayyam* was a great favourite in the late-night philosophy sessions in the House bathroom). He was one of those midges; spinning, dancing, caught in a sudden draught, lifted up, cast down, an insignificant willy-nilly whirligig designed only to bite and be bitten, whose only significance was to be part of a meaningless orthopteric minuet.

'"As flies to wanton boys are we to the gods,"' he said, quoting another set book. '"They kill us for their sport."'

'Eh, that's good, that is,' said Jackie, looming up behind him, 'I like that an' all. And talking of wanton boys, 'ave yer seen my young lass?'

'Your young lass, Jackie? You mean Isobel.'

'Aye, the little 'un.'

'Isn't she a bit too young for you, Jackie?'

'Of course she is, you daft lummox, but beggars can't be choosers. I'm not to kiss her until we're married.'

174

'You'll have to wait a few years, then, Jackie.'

'Oh aye, but I'm in no hurry. Kissing's like bobbing for apples, and I were never much good at that.'

'The thing is, Jackie,' said Freddie, 'I think they've kept her in.'

The giant was genuinely shocked.

'Kept her in, kept her in? On a night like this? You wouldn't keep a gnat in on a night like this. It's the first decent night we've had since thingummebob. That's criminal, that is. Poor little lass. I'll go in and let her out.'

Freddie was beginning to understand Isobel's soft spot for Jackie, but he felt Jackie's latest suggestion might be counter-productive.

'I wouldn't do that, Jackie.'

'Why ever not?'

'Well, they think you're a bit . . . unruly . . . you know . . . to be going out with a thirteen-year-old. If you go barging in, it might sort of confirm their worst fears.'

'Eh, well, what do you suggest?'

'Send Mrs Aylott a present,' suggested Freddie. 'Suck up to her.'

'Present, let me see now. I'd give her one of the boats,' said Jackie. 'She could have *Westminster Bridge*, but they 'in't mine. They all belong to t'bank. And they'll soon belong to t'Bembows. Bembows'll own everything around here. And now they're like to own Flagg Foot. It's going to be a Bembow Holiday Hamlet. Bembow, Bembow, what you goin' to do-io?' he broke into a grotesque double bass. 'So what'm I going to give her?'

'Send her some flowers,' suggested Freddie.

'Eh, that's a good notion. I'll pick 'em in t'churchyard now.'

Freddie watched him lumber off into the twilight to plunder the Michaelmas daisies.

26

It was the morning of the eighth day.

The appalling Leacock was in the dining room again when they made their appearance five minutes after the regulation hour for breakfast. Bertrand had spent an unconscionable time in the lav, doubtless with a bout of constipaggers as a result of all the Flat Foot food he hadn't been eating. Freddie was suffering a bit himself.

There was something oddly conniving about Leacock, Freddie had decided. It was as though he knew, or thought he knew, your innermost parts. It was the last thing Freddie wanted first thing in the morning.

'How do, young 'uns?' said Leacock. 'Wish I could laze in bed like you. Isn't that right, Mrs A?'

Mrs Aylott had come in bearing tea and her usual air of abstraction. She set the tea down and poured some out for Freddie – a service, he was pleased to see, that she omitted to do for Leacock.

'I'm late myself this morning. Mr Aylott's gone into town again, and I had to see to the goats. Haddock suit you, boys?'

Freddie didn't really care for haddock, and fish anyway had been done a disservice as a category by the pilchards of the previous evening. Freddie explained what haddock was to Bertrand, who closed his eyes and went slightly green.

'The haddock is out of this world,' enthused Leacock. 'Come to England and not eat haddock? You might as well stay at home and scoff your horsemeat, young Frenchie. Come on, what's your name, you show him.'

'My name's Freddie,' said Freddie.

'You show him, Freddie.'

'I made it special,' said Mrs Aylott. 'Mr Aylott brought it back from Whitehaven last night.'

'Oh, all right, thank you,' said Freddie, despising himself but feeling sorry for Mrs Aylott.

'And I'll have another slab for mese'n,' said Leacock. 'Give me the Frenchie's portion.'

It smelt, when it arrived, much as Freddie had feared, and came in massive slimy chunks bathed in a watery milky fluid that tasted of weewee.

Bertrand ate his toast perfunctorily, muttered something about his migraine, and went back to the bedroom. Freddie continued to pick at his fish, hoping that Leacock would finish quickly and leave. Indeed, Leacock did eat at enormous speed, swilling great wedges of haddock down among succulent mouthfuls of tea. When he had finished, he mopped the weewee up with his bread, pushed his plate away, gurked, and sat back with all the air of a man who intends to talk.

Freddie felt as trapped by his plateful of haddock as if by physical bonds. At his preparatory school, you were beaten if you didn't eat your food. Its legacy was to make you view the approach of an unpalatable dish with the same sort of doom-laden fascination as a rabbit watching an advancing car.

'Now then, young 'un. What have you been getting up to? Not much lady-killing round here, though you're welcome to a bra and pantie set in peach-blush Bri-Nylon fresh in from the works in Pontefract. Their gift value is such they'd make little Bo-Peep open her legs for you.'

Freddie swallowed a tiny piece of fibrous fish the wrong way.

'I know,' said Leacock, thumping his back, 'one gasps

at the notion of the thing. But wait till you see the genuine article in the boot of my Vanguard. Better now?'

'All right now,' whimpered Freddie.

'So what've you been up to. Boating?'

'Yes.'

'That's Bembows' boathouse now, as good as. Have they got plans for this place? Bembow, Bembow, so much for you to do-io . . . You been round the Hall, I hear. Oh yes, I know everything that goes on. Part of the job. You can't sell underwear if you don't know what's going on ha-ha. But I can tell you now, since you look like a clever little perisher. They send me in first when they have a place in mind. I check it out, do the unpopular things that have to be done so no mud sticks. I am the man in mufti. I wear many hats. You been up to the Hall! We've got that in our sights. You been on that little steamer? Have we got eyes on the little steamer! I know everything si'thee, just see if I don't. Why, they're acquiring this very place. Where we sit now eating haddock, you know that? Got themselves into Queer Street. But that's by the by.'

Freddie pushed away his plate. He wasn't obliged to sit here and listen to this.

'Not hungry?' enquired Mr Leacock, preparing to take over his haddock as if it were a lakeside property.

'Not hungry. Just feeling rather sick.'

27

Freddie looked in on Bertrand, who was lying in bed looking sick in his own beautiful way with a white face and doleful expression.

'Are you all right?'

'I shall be OK. I sometimes have this migraine for two days. I will be all right later.'

'I'm going over to the boathouse.'

But when he arrived, he found Mr Seathwaite lying on his bed asleep with a look on his face that defied arousing.

The prospect of a whole day with nothing to do made him master his customary diffidence, and he walked back up the path to Hell Hall.

He found Mrs Seathwaite in the garden. She made a dramatically tragic figure with her white face and her dark glasses and her hat.

'Hullo, Freddie,' she said. 'Where's Bertrand?'

He told her.

'I'm so sorry,' she said. 'He probably needs a powder. My nieces have come back. Perhaps you'd like a ride? You'll find them up at the stables.'

Freddie trudged up in the direction she had indicated, and found two girls doing something intricate in a saddle room.

They were big girls – Freddie thought seventeen and sixteen – not much older than him – but big and scornful and grownup.

They seemed not in the least interested in having a schoolboy foisted on them. If anything, the younger one, Diana, was even less interested than her sister Elizabeth.

When Freddie told them their aunt had sent him up for a ride, they rolled their eyes.

'Typical Aunt,' said Diana.

'You can't ride in those,' said Elizabeth, pointing at his shorts.

'It's all right, really,' said Freddie. 'I don't really want to ride particularly.'

'Not want to ride?' said Diana, as if he were some kind of a freak. 'Why did you come up here, then?'

'Well. I would ride if . . . if there were a pony.'

'The only pony we've got is Puffin and he's got sore hocks.'

'I see,' said Freddie, preparing to withdraw. 'All right. Thank you.'

'But you could have Major.'

'Oh. Right.'

'Major's about eighteen hands.'

'Oh.'

Something was snorting in a far stable. They led it out. It was an enormous grey the size of a haystack.

'I suppose you've ridden before,' said Diana.

Freddie had ridden before but not very much. His relations with horses were based on mutual distrust, but he didn't like to seem a complete wet to these scornful hoydens.

They saddled Major for him, and he hoisted himself on board. It was like sitting on a mountain. The girls leapt on two other steeds, and the little cortège moved off through a gate and down a long stony track.

The girls became distantly conversational.

'Aunt says we're sort of related,' said Diana. 'But I've never heard of you.'

'Oh,' said Freddie, nervously.

He could sense Major heaving mettlesomely beneath him.

'He'll be all right when he's had a run,' said Elizabeth, judiciously. 'What d'you think of Hell Hall? Bit of a hoot, actually.'

'Does your uncle live down at the boathouse?'

'Most of the time. He's a sort of inventor, really. He's had lots of ideas. He even had a record company called Hell's Bells. Then there was his telephonevision. He's a bit short of cash now. Poor Uncle has awful luck. Just as well Aunt's got some. Cash, I mean.'

'Does she always wear black?' asked Freddie.

'Of course. She's in mourning for Jojo.'

'Oh. Was he your cousin?'

'Good God, no. He was a bit of a dog, actually.'

So that was whom Bertrand reminded her of!

'She's a great believer in reincarnation, though. She's always expecting Jojo to turn up.'

'What sort of dog was he?' he asked.

'A French poodle, I expect.'

Freddie threw back his head and laughed. A poodle! Poor Bertrand.

'I say, look out.'

They had arrived at an open gate where the track branched off onto a large field of rough pasture. Major, seizing the opportunity, suddenly shot off at full speed, accelerating from walk to gallop quicker than a Healey Silverstone.

Freddie suddenly realized why Major was called Major; galloping was his particular forte.

Freddie had never really galloped before. Cantering seemed an altogether more lenient way to travel.

'Pull his head up,' shouted the girls, but Major had the bit between his teeth.

Round the field Major flew, with Freddie hanging on for dear life. Never had he seen grass whizz by so fast. Somehow being on a horse at thirty miles an hour was quite different from a car, in fact Freddie would rather have been in car at a hundred and thirty miles an hour.

'Pull him round, get his head up.'

'I can't do anything,' shrieked Freddie.

The horse must have had a mouth like a nutcracker. He seemed entirely impervious in what should have been his most sensitive parts. They had obviously been feeding him on oats all his life.

Freddie caught a glimpse of the girls rolling their eyes and generally indicating irritation with his incompetence; what was happening certainly wasn't their fault.

Major, having circled the field three times, clearly had his mind on higher things for, instead of going for a fourth circuit, he suddenly went full tilt at the most enormous eighteen-barred gate that led out onto beckoning moorland.

'Oh fuck,' shouted Freddie.

'Major,' shouted the girls, almost as though they were urging the beast to make the prodigious jump.

But Major in the end decided he was only a galloping Major, not a jumping General or a leaping Lieutenant, and stopped dead about three yards from the gate.

Freddie flew over his head and landed very hard on his bottom.

'Are you all right?' asked Elizabeth.

'You shouldn't have let his head go down,' said Diana.

'Shit,' said Freddie.

Major unleashed a quantity of steaming excrement.

It was the first command of Freddie's that he had obeyed.

28

The girls accompanied him with considerable ill-grace as he led Major back to the stables on foot. After the rituals of unsaddling, they deposited him at the front door of Hell Hall, leaving him on the steps while they went inside, presumably to report to Mrs Seathwaite.

Freddie sat on the cold stone nursing his bottom. He didn't like to go in while they told her what a weed he'd been.

She came out full of solicitude as the girls returned to the stables.

'Such brutes, horses. Dogs are far more intelligent.'

She pressed him to stay and play the piano while she made some tea. He addressed himself gingerly to the Bechstein on the horsehair piano-stool but after a quick 'God moves in a mysterious way', and a stab at the four flats of 'Immortal, Invisible' he was grateful for the lenient springing of the sofa. Mrs Seathwaite came in bearing tea and chocolate digestives on a silver tray. She settled herself beside him while he ate. He could smell just a hint of the softly troubling perfume that seemed to be a natural distillation exhaled by her white skin.

'Talking of dogs,' she said, 'my niece Diana says she told you about my dog.'

'Your dog?'

'You know . . . the poodle.'

'Oh. Oh yes.'

'He was a very dear dog. French, you know. Like Bertrand. So intelligent. You believe in reincarnation?'

'Well, I . . .'

'I know. A healthy scepticism. He had exactly Bertrand's eyes.'

Why was she telling him all this? It was as though she wanted to underline something.

'I just thought you ought to know,' she said. 'Poor Jojo. Such a tragedy. Of course he didn't have to drown. Somebody could have saved him.'

'I'm sorry,' he murmured, not knowing what else to say. 'How absolutely awful.' His mother had a good line in soothing social noises, and it seemed to work now.

When he got back to Flat Foot, he found Bertrand had gone out. He extracted his Wordsworth and tried to read in the Res Lounge, piling cushions under his sore buttock, and feeling sorry for himself.

Bertrand didn't come in until almost teatime.

'Where've you been?' he asked him.

But the pretty face was as elusive as ever.

'I went for a promenade,' he said.

'A rather long promenade.'

Freddie had the strangest feeling that he had been visiting the boathouse.

The bruise on his bottom came up in the most dramatic greens and blues, he found later, when he examined himself in the lav. But he was damned if he was going to show it to Bertrand.

29

As it happened, it was a different affliction that greeted him in the morning.

Freddie had had indications of an emergent spot for a couple of days now. There was a tender area above the right eyebrow.

He had applied a generous dollop of Valderma, but he had learned by experience that if a spot had a mind to emerge, there was no medicament on earth that would halt it in its course.

> 'Ne oyntement that wolde clense and byte,
> That him mighte helpen of hys whelkes white,
> Nor of the knobbes sittinge on his cheeks . . .'

Spots were one of Freddie's particular horrors, so he had striven vigorously to contain it, and yesterday the thing had seemed reasonably under control, simply throbbing a little and bulging redly below the surface. Occasionally they did that and went away. But this morning as he did a reflex frown at the grey daylight on awakening and felt the tell-tale tenderness, he knew the worst had happened.

He wasn't going to go and see the Seathwaites today, that was certain.

At least it wasn't raining and the clouds were high, and his buttock seemed, in spite of its lurid colour, to be no longer sore but merely made of cardboard.

'Today,' he said to Bertrand at breakfast, 'today we climb Stickletop. We have to do it before we leave.'

He kept his spotty side away from the light as he spoke so that Bertrand would not make the connection between this decision and his deformity. Besides he did not want to put Bertrand off his bacon with glimpses of his pulsating shagger.

He was almost glad to note that the familiar self-loathing and sense of pariahness that a spot induced also served a little to quench his ardour.

'D'accord,' said Bertrand. 'Will it be a long promenade?'

'Four or five hours, I should think.'

Isobel entered with the teapot, and Freddie cocked his spot still further into shadow.

'Could we have our packed lunch quite soon, please? We're going to climb Stickletop,' he said sidelong.

'It's no good hiding your boil under a bushel,' she replied. 'I can see it just fine, it's red enough to light a path in the dark.'

'Go and jump in the lake,' rejoined Freddie, piqued, 'there's plenty of it to choose from. Really a puddle would do for a little squirt like you.'

'Mind you don't squeeze it too hard, pus-bag. There might be nothing left of you.'

She retreated rather fast with the empty cornflakes packet.

Later, Mr Aylott peered round the door.

'The forecast said rain this evening, lads. If you're going up Stickletop, keep to the path, see, and make sure you come down in good time. I'm not going up after you, we've enough to do down here.'

Freddie was almost tempted to change his mind, but the thought of mooching around all day down here with the right side of his face turned away from Bertrand made him resolute. He was already conscious of a slightly stiff neck.

On the mountain, he could walk ahead or behind or on the right of the boy, with his collar turned up high round his ears; the cool wind would soothe, the soft rain, if it came, would help to heal.

'Better take your map. You can read a map? Be here sharp for tea, mind.'

Freddie's school's Combined Cadet Force prided itself in its map-reading instruction. Apart from a tendency to confuse boundaries with paths, Freddie was adequately proficient. The map was stowed into his coat pocket while the tongue sandwiches, chocolate biscuit and baby Kümmel went into the haversack.

Their route took them up the same track towards Muckle Pass that they had followed some days earlier, but instead of branching round to the right and up the hill, they crossed a stile and walked up through a little valley busy with the noise of its stream. It led them into a small copse.

A large animal suddenly leapt across their path.

'Wha . . .' said Freddie.

'It is a, how you say, a chevreuil?' said Bertrand, not in the least alarmed.

As the beast cantered away between the trees, Freddie could see that it was indeed some kind of deer. His mother would have spoken of it with enthusiasm and told you how you could know it by its markings; that it was a roe or a red or a fallow, and doubtless Wordsworth would have done too, but Freddie was less interested in its make than its symbolism. It registered a note of wildness again, of danger in the enterprise, of sudden natural forces that were beyond his conjecture or control. The huge grey sweep of mountain ahead of them could easily hide a troll or a bloody-bones.

187

They climbed on past fallen trees and over little water-falls, until the firs thinned and another stile appeared. Here they paused and gazed out at the wilderness beyond.

First, there was an enormously large undulating bog. Beyond were the scree-studded foothills and flanks of Stickletop itself. (They were approaching from the south-west.) The spiky-edged summit was just touched with a little fluffy cloudlet like a marshmallow but the rest of the mountain was plainly visible.

'It's about 3,000 feet,' said Freddie, 'that's around 1,000 metres.'

He knew that the peak was puny beside Mont Blanc but he was at the same time proud of the undoubted magnitude of the British spectacle.

He was so proud, indeed, that he forgot to hide his spot, and hurriedly turned his gaze as if to inspect a distant peak, but Bertrand didn't seem to mind.

'I have the boutons sometimes,' he said, though Freddie didn't believe him. 'I like boutons. I think they make the visage more cheeryful.'

Bertrand himself seemed in a more cheeryful mood today, and Freddie – apart from the odd twinge – could put the spot entirely out of his mind.

The way ahead of them was daunting. Apart from the difficulty of following the track across the bog which looked so clear on the map but on the ground seemed to dissolve into three or four equally unconvincing possibili-ties, the mountain itself seemed so awfully large.

Freddie recalled the little church in the village – where Jackie said he was going to pick flowers. Well, some of those flowers were doubtless decorating the graves of climbers and walkers who lay there.

A chilly gust blew straight across the bog at them, straight from Stickletop's prickly summit. Freddie shiv-ered, but he could not possibly turn back. His shagger gave a little squirt of pain at the notion of the loss of face involved.

Amid an upspringing of skylarks, they set out across the squelchy desolation, aiming – where the path seemed to deviate – for a track that could be seen traversing one of the lower slopes half a mile away.

Their path doubled, disappeared, revived, doubled again, sometimes leading them through marsh of alarming colour and viscosity. At one point, they hit upon a long, narrow, dry shoulder of ground that led them nearly all the way to their goal, only to dash their hopes with a moat-like morass at its end. They retraced their steps to the middle of the moor, and started again. At length, they emerged mud-splattered and hot.

The wind had died, and a pale self-congratulatory sun came out rather in the manner of Sir Cuthbert Bewdley, 'Ponger' Bewdley's father, who was something in the City and one of the School Governors.

Freddie suggested leaving their heavy coats at the base of the mountain, but Bertrand demurred.

'It could make cold at the sommit,' he said.

It was now half past eleven. They had been going for over an hour. They rested and plodded on.

The track took them up a steep little valley between two ridges, strewn with rocks and boulders, and divided by a miniature ravine. One or two bleak little thorn bushes nestled in the lee of the slope.

A mine must have been worked here once, for they passed a brick-fringed cavity in the hillside with fragments of unrecognizable machinery rusting outside.

Apart from this and the occasional hopeless-looking sheep, there were no signs of life. Even the birds had disappeared. Freddie peeped into the bricky cavity and peeped out again, fearing a dark denizen.

At the top of the valley there was, inevitably, another

slope, this time traversing one of the mountain's mighty flanks at a near forty-five-degree angle. Above them, intermittently, they could see the beetling peak of the Stickle.

Once the next ridge was surmounted, the path split three ways, with a deceptive sheep-track branching out on its own. They could now begin to see the great expanse of the lake stretched out below.

Stickletop's top still looked a long way off.

The path they chose led, almost vertically, straight up beside a tumbling watercourse that spattered and spouted and jetted and jabbered on its way to join the Mare Tranquillitatis of Ettenwater.

> 'Calms appear when storms are past,
> Love will have his hour at last,'

thought Freddie.

Were all his confusions going to end in fulfilment? He could hardly think so. Bertrand was a creature apart, not to be touched. The very notion of wanting to branded him as untouchable. All he could touch was himself, and that didn't seem to provide anything more than a source of friction and a sense of not liking himself very much. And if you didn't like yourself very much, whom could you expect to like you?

These thoughts ran through his mind as they sat and looked out across the spectacular scene below. Nature was supposed to make you feel elevated by its grandeur, Freddie thought, not worry about tossing.

They had been heated by the climb but now Stickle's breezes put a stop to all steaminess. There was a distinct nip in the air.

'Allez,' said Bertrand, 'we must use the beau temps.'

He had been on the mountain in bad weather, he told Freddie, and it was not droll.

190

They started up the path beside the water, occasionally splattered by its headlong boundings. It was the hardest walk Freddie had ever undertaken. The path was slippery, and strewn with uneven rocks and stones. As they slowly moved higher, his sense of complete isolation increased. Every hundred yards or so, they had to pause and gasp for breath.

The watercourse seemed if anything bigger and more exuberant, the higher they progressed.

'There's a tarn at the top,' said Freddie, consulting his map, 'and then there's the assault on the summit.'

'I do not like this Tickletop.'

Freddie half hoped that it meant Bertrand wanted to turn back but it seemed it was only a Gallic grumble because he stood up almost immediately he'd said it, and struck on upwards.

A ditty from one of his mother's old song-books kept recurring in Freddie's mind as he followed the slim brown legs up the ravine:

'A hermit who dwells in these solitudes crossed me,
As way-worn and faint up the mountain I pressed,
The aged man leant on his staff to accost me,
And offered his cell as my mansion of rest.
"Oh no, gentle father, as onward I rove,
No rest but the grave for the pilgrim of love."'

The path came to an abrupt halt as a shoulder of rock appeared, barring the right-hand side of the bank. There was nothing for it but to cross to the boulder-strewn further bank where the water scooted past a minor landslip.

It was hazardous crossing (more hazardous still, Freddie thought, in the dark or if the cloud came down), but eventually they were over and struggling through loose earth and rock towards a last rampart of boulders over which the water zoomed at a furious lick.

At last, even this last obstacle was cleared, and they peered over into a huge dark Grendel lake, deathly still and icy cold, where no birds sang.

Beyond it, the Stickle brooded in jagged isolation.

They sat exhausted, looking out over the best view in the world.

'Shall we have lunch here or at the top?' Freddie asked at length, the beauty of the scene going to his gastric juices. It was now a quarter to one. The clouds were still high and the sun twinkled jubilantly between them.

'At the top,' said Bertrand. 'Au sommet.'

They got up and walked round the tarn to where the track arrowed up amid a desolation of tumultuous dusty-grey scree.

Half an hour later, rounding a little outcrop that edged the skyline, they found themselves walking up a narrow spine of rock which led up and up to a tiny clearing centred with a heap of stones.

This was Stickletop itself.

Suddenly the exposed nature of their position struck Freddie like a visitation of madness. He looked round, and all he could see was air, cloud and chasm; and the further he walked up, the more tenuous the earth seemed to be.

The very force of gravity might suddenly go into abeyance. He stopped, giddy and paralysed. Eternity seemed to whirl about him, clutching at his strings.

'What is the matter, Freddie?'

Bertrand had stopped and was watching him with concern.

'I don't know. It's . . .'

'It is le vertige.'

'Whatever it is, it's stupid.'

192

Freddie was ashamed of his weakness in front of Bertrand but the French boy shrugged.

'C'est normale. I have this feeling. We stop now?'

But, having admitted the problem, Freddie felt better. Cautiously advancing, holding onto the rock wall as he went, almost on all fours, he seated himself beside Bertrand with his back against the cairn and looked down.

Far below, the curved expanse of the lake glistened like his mother's silver salamander brooch between the tweedy greys and greens of the shoreline. On either side, crumpled hills rose, layer upon layer. Above, the sky provided its own illimitable soft material. Only towards its lower edge, to the west, did it appear to be made of harder, more metallic-seeming stuff. As he looked, Freddie realized it was not grey sky at all but distant shimmering sea.

Neither of the boys spoke. Only the wind provided its low commentary.

> '"So in a season of calm weather
> Though inland far we be
> Our souls have sight of that immortal sea
> Which brought us hither,"'

said Freddie finally.

'Uh?' said Bertrand.

'Wordsworth,' said Freddie.

'Virdsvirth?'

The name was unpronounceable in French.

'The one you're not descended from. He would have liked this; in fact he probably did like this. He probably sat here,' said Freddie.

'He would probably have got cold derrière,' said Bertrand, shifting his little round shanks. 'But I like this place. It makes all clean.'

'Yes,' agreed Freddie. 'Did you ever do Vergil?'

193

'Vergil? Oui, bien sûr, Vergil.'

'It's when Aeneas goes into the Underworld, and there's a bit where old Father Anchises is telling him what happens to the souls of the dead, how the divine spark has to be washed clean, and they're sort of hung out to dry for ages in the vast and empty winds. Well, it's like that up here.'

'Yes,' said Bertrand, 'I like these fast and empty winds.'

One construction of man, Freddie noticed, standing out amid all the labours of nature. Two tall thin towers, flanked by a huddle of lesser buildings, squatted by the sea that brought us hither, their pale concrete walls and geometric shape outlined clearly against the natural irregularities of the landscape.

Freddie's mother hated things like ribbon developments and holiday camps and caravan parks; and factories were high on her list of disfavour. He thought of her disapproval now, and wondered what such a place should be doing among these lonesome vales.

A little plume of vapour wafted from one of the buildings as they watched, like smoke from a resting dragon or miasma from a necromancer's castle.

Freddie found the place on the map.

'Ettenmouth,' he said. 'It means monster's mouth.'

'C'est juste,' said Bertrand.

The boys ate their sandwiches, and the chocolate biscuit and the orange, and they washed them down with fizzy lemonade and Kümmel swigs. And then, because the wind had started to freshen, they set off down the path again with many a backward glance at the god's-eye view.

As they descended, the sky grew darker. Fingers of cloud started to tickle the summit behind them, and the sun joined the rest of the School Governors behind closed doors. The weather forecast, it seemed, was in arrears.

By the time they reached the tarn it had started to rain,

which made the path down the watercourse more and more slippery. Bertrand skidded and nearly fell into the foaming torrent but was stopped by Freddie who lunged out and grabbed him by the haversack.

'Merci à toi, Freddie.'

'You'd have gone like Clementine.'

'Comment?'

'"Oh my darling, oh my darling,"' carolled Freddie, and slipped on a greasy boulder, Bertrand catching him in turn.

They were both still slightly drunk on the god's-eye view and the Kümmel, but when they reached the bottom they were sobered by the sight of the cloud which was chasing them down from the top.

Visions of desperate lungings about in the mist, falling into bogs, tumbling over precipices, began to fill Freddie's excitable imagination. They were still a long way from the lakeside. He opened the map and scanned it anxiously for inspiration.

'Look,' he said to Bertrand, his brow clearing, 'we can take this path. It'll get us down quicker. We went the long way round before.'

He pointed to a dotted track which at length led down to the lane near Flat Foot.

'When we're there, we'll be able to follow the road. And look, there's a barn or something marked halfway down. We can always shelter there.'

They set off, skirting the expanse of bogland which they had traversed before, but already the mist was upon them. It had come with astonishing speed in prescribed Lakeland manner, and they were soon peering through the wet swirliness at landmarks which had been plain as a Langdale pikestaff before.

Luckily, the path was easy to follow, running past a low stone wall, through a little wood, and out onto an expanse of coarse grass where, caught in the open, they felt the full force of the rain.

'There,' cried Freddie, seeing a dark squarish shape looming over a brow, 'that must be the barn I saw on the map. Let's shelter in there for a bit.'

But when they drew closer, they saw it wasn't a barn but a Nissen hut, a cluster of Nissen huts, in fact. It reminded Freddie of the Army Camp he'd been to last year. There was still some barbed wire around the perimeter and a Strictly No Admittance, WD Property, notice, but it was faded, broken and rusty.

They approached the first hut cautiously, just in case it might still be in use, but the door had been broken and the windows smashed. They entered, grateful to be out of the wind, and took off their haversacks.

'It must be from the war,' said Freddie. 'They probably used the moor for exercises.'

He had already been to a couple of Camps with the school Corps and thought very little of them. His brother said it helped you get a Commission for your National Service, which was absolutely de rigueur; but it still seemed a waste of holidays.

Freddie had one more little bottle in his haversack – a Highland Queen whisky – and he unearthed it. The moment seemed entirely appropriate.

'Here,' he said, offering it to Bertrand, 'have first swig.'

They wandered round the hut taking miniature swigs and examining the dilapidations. Various spiders had taken up residence, there was a great deal of splintered glass, and various initials and graffiti were still discernible on the walls.

'What is CUNT?' asked Bertrand.

Freddie blushed stupidly.

'It's er what girls have.'

196

'Ah. It is the same as we say, con. I think it is a mysterious opprobrium.'

Freddie was pleased with the remark.

'You surprise me sometimes, Bertrand.'

'In the war, even the childrens learned to be discreet.'

Freddie wanted to ask what life was like under the Germans, but he didn't like to hurt French pride. He looked at some more graffiti.

'B.Y. loves J.B. 1944,' he said. 'I wonder who they were.'

While he spoke, he idly scratched B.V. and F.R.A.P. on two ends of a heart, and transfixed it with an arrow. He didn't really mean Bertrand to see, but he came over just at the wrong moment.

'Why you do that, Freddie?'

Then, if ever, was the moment to tell him. But Freddie blushed like a radish and said:

'It was a joke. A . . . a drôlerie . . .'

'Oh . . . I see. A good joke, hein?'

Sensing that the rain was slackening, Freddie seized on the opportunity to escape his bêtise. They put on their haversacks and emerged again. The cloud was still drifting among the huts, making them look like spectral barges.

As they walked betwen them, Freddie plodding in front – the embarrassment in the hut had made his shagger start throbbing – he noticed a light shining from one of the windows. He turned back to Bertrand, finger to lip, and they crept up for closer inspection.

The hut in question seemed in better order than the rest, as though someone had lavished some care on its upkeep. It had a door, and glass in its windows.

The boys gingerly raised their heads to the sill and peered over. The most unexpected tableau rewarded their inspection.

Inside, warmed by the glow from an old army stove with its there-was-a-crooked-man chimney pipe, stood Mr

Leacock in a raincoat. He was stooped over a table on which various portions of what looked like earth and twigs and grass were arrayed. It could hardly be that he was making a Wordsworthian collection of rocks and stones and trees, or that he was simply undertaking an exercise in pure botany. Mr Leacock was not that sort of person.

What then could he be doing?

The other odd thing was that Mr Leacock didn't look at all like the underwear salesman, unpleasant though he was, no stranger to the Flat Foot dining room. He seemed now to become someone altogether more menacing and purposeful.

It was only when he paused for a moment to pick his nose that the impression was broken, and the Man in Mufti turned back into the Leacock they knew and loathed.

'I think,' whispered Bertrand, 'Monsieur Leacock will not be presenting himself for his pilchard tonight.'

30

For the next four days, the weather kept up a sporadic foggy drizzle, and the spot slowly subsided. The boys' regime followed a consistent pattern.

In the morning, they would read, or walk, or read and walk. Sometimes, in their excursions, they would see the wild figures of the Seathwaite girls on their ponies, flying into a forest or poised on a ravine.

For lunch, the boys went to Hell Hall at Mrs Seathwaite's insistence. The girls were out all day, she said, and she was glad of the company.

Freddie knew whose company she was really glad of, but there was nowhere else for him to go. He had made his feelings plain about horses after the Major interlude, and doubtless the girls had made theirs plain about him.

Even though Freddie had the feeling of being de trop as far as Mrs Seathwaite was concerned, now that he knew the nature of her infatuation for Bertrand he was inclined to feel less jealous. An attractive woman searching for a transmigrated soul was infinitely less worrying than one who went hell-bent for the body. Although the Chaplain had always indicated that souls were more important than bodies, in adult life it didn't seem to work out that way.

Freddie had not passed on to Bertrand what he learned from the girls about their aunt's obsession. He thought it might make the boy affronted to be told he was regarded as the reincarnation of a pooch; but he found it a comfort from time to time to reflect on the truth of the matter as

Mrs Seathwaite gave Bertrand the best pieces from the joint and the biggest helping of summer pudding.

After lunch, they progressed to the drawing room where Freddie knew that, once again, he was to be stationed at the piano after they had eaten their chocolates and drunk their coffee.

Freddie understood when it was time – an inflection of the voice, almost a little clearing of the throat, an adjustment of the dark glasses – and he would get up and go over to the Bechstein and run his fingers through the key of A Major, before settling down to the wonderful John Bacchus Dykes, who had fallen foul of the Bishop of Durham for writing such enjoyable hymn tunes – St Bees and 'Holy, Holy, Holy', and 'Eternal Father, Strong to Save' and St Fulbert – or perhaps Toplady's 'Rock of Ages' – or the great Hanover 'O Worship the King'.

He would just discern them stealing out, and then they would be gone for an hour and a half or so.

'Where do you go?' asked Freddie later.

'Oh, she walks me down to the water, or up to the hills. She say they are the favourite promenades. She say she like to see me run.'

'And do you?'

'Bien sûr. Why not? Sometimes she throws sticks and stones. I say to her, you should have a dog.'

'And what does she say to that?'

'She say to me there is only one dog for her. I do not know what she means. She talk about the afterlife, and the voyage of the soul. And then she ask me if there are rabbits in the Champs-Elysées, the how you say Elysium Fields. Of course there are no rabbits in the Champs-Elysées. It is in the middle of Paris. But she look so disappointed when I say no rabbits that I say maybe, in fact I say there are definitely rabbits in the Champs-Elysées, I was making a plaisanterie, I tell her, and she look so happy.'

'That was very nice of you, Bertrand.'

'She is crazy, I think, but c'est normale, she is English. She make us a good déjeuner so one can excuse much. If she likes me to curl up on the end of her bed while she reads her periodical, it is no great hardship for me. What else could one do on such a day? Ping-pong? One must indulge the eccentric or one must cultivate ennui.'

Freddie had never heard Bertrand spout so much in one go. He was impressed with the boy's Gallic acceptance of the unfathomable oddity of life. It was something from which he, Freddie, could learn. What he burned for was inadmissible and could never be enjoyed. The only course was a philosophical acceptance of his own.

It was interesting, in passing, to note that Bertrand did not after all seem to mind being taken for a dog.

31

On the third day spent in this manner, Freddie had become impatient. The night before he had had a dream in which he had been in bed with Mrs Seathwaite and Bertrand – a most shameful and pleasurable affair – and it had left him full of desire for her. It was exciting to know someone's innermost parts without them knowing that you knew.

Bertrand being out of the room for so long was bad enough, but wanting them both made it almost intolerable.

When they both finally showed up, Freddie had exhausted the solaces of the Bechstein, and was ready for a showdown.

'Time for tea before you go back,' said Mrs Seathwaite gaily. 'Got some doughnuts in the village this morning.'

'I don't want any tea,' muttered Freddie darkly, 'thank you.'

His spot had started to throb again.

'No tea? But you must have tea. Are you feeling all right?'

She moved nearer to him. He could feel the delicious feminine waft of her legs under her skirt, he could smell the scent she used. Tears of desire and unhappiness welled up in his eyes. She looked round at Bertrand.

'Why don't you go on back to Flagg Foot, Bertrand? You say you never understand English teatime anyway.'

'OK,' he shrugged. 'D'accord.'

He went out of the French windows, suitably enough,

and Freddie watched him disappear round the corner of the terrace near the bee-loud buddleia.

Mrs Seathwaite said nothing.

At length he turned, cautiously keeping his spot as much as possible in shadow.

'All right,' she said finally. 'I think it's time you and I had a little talk. Tell me, what exactly is the matter?

'Nothing.'

'No, come on, Freddie, I want to know.'

'Nothing. Really nothing.'

'I don't believe that.'

'I . . . I'm in love with you.'

There, he had said it. Words he could never use to Bertrand and could scarcely use to a woman of forty. How on earth had he had the courage? Even as he closed his mouth, he was aghast. What would she do? Make him wash his mouth out with carbolic? Forbid him to come again? Tell his mother and Rollo?

'Oh, Freddie,' said Mrs Seathwaite.

'I know I'm too young,' said Freddie, 'but I feel it inside me.'

He did feel it too, in the stomach, like going back to school when he was a little boy but 'sweet, sweet, sweet, O Pan', instead of the sour hopelessness of beginning of term.

'What are we to do with you, Freddie? I had no idea.'

'I sit here playing hymns while you're with Bertrand.'

'I thought you liked hymns.'

'I couldn't bear it, thinking of you both.'

'You mean . . . you thought Bertrand and I were . . .?'

He nodded dumbly.

'I'm sorry,' he mumbled. 'I'd better go.'

He rose to leave, but to his surprise, she leant over and stopped him.

'No, Freddie. It's all right.'

They sat looking at each other. The sky had darkened again and the wind was driving rose petals in pale flibber-tigibbets across the lawn.

Mrs Seathwaite looked at him intently as she lit a cigarette.

'You like Bertrand, don't you,' she said. 'I mean, really like.'

So she knew about it!

'I wasn't sure about anything until I fell in love with you too,' he said. 'I thought I might be a homo. I had dreams about Bertrand.'

Mrs Seathwaite laughed.

'I'm sorry,' said Freddie huffily. 'I didn't mean it to be such a joke.'

'Don't be upset, Freddie. We have to laugh at ourselves sometimes.'

'I don't understand.'

'Perhaps you will one day. You're a sweet boy but there are things you . . . Bertrand is not what he seems, you know.'

Freddie felt suddenly terribly ashamed, it was all in his mind. She really did think Bertrand was a reincarnation.

'You mean . . . he's a dog?'

'A spirit who has been a dog, on its way to a higher realization? Perhaps that is the best way of putting it.'

He did not raise the subject with her again. Nor did he dwell upon that wonderful wound he had discovered in his dream between her legs.

Perhaps he too was somebody else's dog. A nasty, dirty, ugly, spotty mongrel.

32

After tea on the fourth Hell Hall lunch day, they deceived Mrs Seathwaite.

It was only a white lie, Freddie told himself, but he was conscious that she would have disapproved.

They told her they were going back to Flat Foot, but in fact they'd hit on the notion of asking Mrs Aylott if they could be out for their evening meal. She didn't mind. It saved her money. It meant the boys could take their packed lunches down to the boathouse for supper.

Mr Seathwaite seemed scarcely aware that any time had elapsed since they last spoke.

'Ah, the youths,' he said. 'Bustle, bustle.'

Through the long late afternoon, they worked slowly over the length of Great-Uncle Gussie's masterpiece, touching up the paint, repairing rents with waterproof glue and twine, and going over the inner tubing (patched together from a fresh supply of rubber sheeting obtained from War Department sources), checking for leaks which they mended with a heavy-duty puncture repair outfit on loan from a local garage.

While they worked, Freddie tried to find out from Mr Seathwaite something of his past, and of how he had come to his particular frame of mind and mode of life.

'The Hall and the estate have always been a millstone around our necks. Poor land, low rents. But we always had great interests in cotton. Of course the war buggered up all that, and the bloody gyppos buggered it up even more. So now we don't have any interests in cotton. In fact we have a great lack of interest in cotton. All we have

205

is Hell Hall and a great deal of bloody hill and water. She,' he jerked his head up at the Hall, 'she doles out as little as she can get away with, mean bitch, they come at me from every side wanting money, they crucify me, you know that? My father would've left me more but he cut me off because I broke an engagement with another girl to marry thingmebob. Interfering old sod, said there was bad blood there, he was right of course. So here I am, assailed on every side, enemies closing in. God knows I've tried, youth. My fingers are work-worn – to the bone, to the bone . . .'

He held up his tobacco-stained hands so that Freddie could inspect his blackened nails. Freddie made one of his mother's soothing noises, but Mr Seathwaite was enjoying himself. He was touching on his favourite subject.

'Things haven't worked out through sheer mischance. I can only put it down to that. Mischance and the malice of others. Even my own brother, who got the money I should have had, even my own brother is a broken reed. Even my own family desert me. When did I last see my children, tell me that? I'll tell you. Yesteryear or bloody nearly. I'll be worms' meat soon. Then they'll be sorry.'

In spite of his gloomy words, Freddie marvelled at the way Mr Seathwaite seemed to have been revived by the project. There was a sparkle in his eye and a spring in his step. The whisky appeared less frequently and even the bullying manner was less in evidence.

33

The next day, Mr Seathwaite produced the monster's head from the back of the boathouse. He brought it out with considerable pride, as well he might, for Great-Uncle Gussie must have been something of an artist. The whole appearance of the thing was shockingly lifelike. Its eyes flashed and its lip drooled. It was only too possible to imagine it couched in its underwater cavern rearing its monstrous brood, or scouring the waters for its dubious nutriment.

'It needs paint, there is a gash in the side of the mouth,' said Mr Seathwaite, 'but when it is done we shall be on the last lap.'

An hour later, it was ready. The aeroplane paint had dried and the fissure in the lower jaw was stitched and coloured. Even the eyes had been touched up to bring out the red of the veins.

'Now for supper, youths. Afterwards we will carry out the final offices.'

Freddie had asked Mrs Aylott for pork pies whenever possible for their packed lunch, knowing Mr Seathwaite's predilection for the things. Now, as with a monster's appetite, he positively wallowed in the slabby pastry, the jellied endoderm, and the peppery little chunks of pinkish gristliness.

'But we must not be greedy, youth. There is someone else who needs the feast more than we do.'

'Who's that, Mr Seathwaite?'

'Little Ettie,' he said, pointing at the monster. 'She must have her morsel.'

'Pork pie?' asked Freddie, noting that Mr Seathwaite was actually keeping some back.

Mr Seathwaite pointed.

'In that dustbin over there, I am collecting suitable titbits for her diet. Finished your supper, youth?'

'Yes,' said Freddie, slurping down the last of his Dundee cake with a sluice of brown ale.

'Have a dekko inside.'

Freddie and Bertrand advanced on the metal bin and opened its lid.

They stepped back as one, with unison dismay, as the most appalling stench in the world leapt like a jack-in-the-box from the interior.

'Mustn't be squeamish, youths. Monster's victuals are strong meat.'

The meat was strong all right. And so was the dead fish, the rotting cabbage, the decomposing pigeon, and the high-as-heaven hare, all discernible among other nameless slushes and fibres within.

Mr Seathwaite strode over with chef-like pride, threw in the piece of pie as if it were the crowning source of spice, and closed the lid once more.

The boys breathed again.

'The brew is young yet,' said Mr Seathwaite, 'but it is working. It will serve. Now, youth, let us stretch Ettie out on the quay and prepare her for a meal.'

The creature was at least thirty feet long by the time she was fully unravelled, and that was still without the head in place.

'Once we have stuffed her maw with the mixture,' said Mr Seathwaite, 'we shall need to seal it.'

Freddie's face was growing longer and longer as he realized the enormity of what he was going to be asked to do. The stench still clung to the hairs of his nostrils.

'We shall seal her with puncture glue,' continued Mr

Seathwaite with relish, 'inserting at the same time our one-way valve. This will prevent over-inflation, and allow Ettie to sink back into the depths once she has exhaled. If we fill her now, she will be ready to rise on Thursday night at nine o'clock. After that, if all is well, we will tow her into position at the southern end of the lake, ready for her appearance before the press at the Regatta. A prime hoax. Now, if you are squeamish, I advise a handkerchief.'

With this, he lugged the dustbin forward over the concrete jetty, motioned to Freddie to hold the lip of the inner tube open where it protruded from the throat, and poured the whole putrescent melange down into the interior, poking at the horrific stragglers with an old broom handle.

Freddie gagged and almost retched into his handkerchief with the intensity of the effluvium, and Bertrand retreated junket-faced towards the open doors.

'If you're going to puke, puke into the tube,' cried Mr Seathwaite impatiently, 'no need to waste anything. Every little helps. Otherwise get a grip on yourself, clean round the aperture – here's some detergent – wipe the surface and I'll apply the valve and glue. Ready?'

'Agurrrgy,' said Freddie through his mask.

The smell subsided as the valve went in and the edges of the glued rubber were clamped around it. The head was sewn into place, with a little aperture for the valve beneath it, and the whole thirty-five feet of the humpy creature was finally ready for immersion.

'It's only eight foot deep here,' said Mr Seathwaite, 'but it'll do for the trials. She'll right herself as she fills with gas, and we can ballast her when she rises if there's any correction needed. Now let's put her in. Are you ready?'

Mr Seathwaite grasped the head, Freddie gathered up

the middle, and Bertrand, his little French nose still suffering from smell-shock, plucked at the tail.

'One, two, three, GO,' shouted Mr Seathwaite.

Ettie sploshed inertly into the water, and settled slowly towards the bottom until they could see no more than a red eye cocked accusingly at them as her head turned over.

'This calls for a drink,' said Mr Seathwaite.

They toasted Ettie in whisky.

'A good evening's work, youths. I shall see you on Thursday.'

'This British hydrogen bomb, lovely device,' said Mr Leacock, guzzling fried bread and brown sauce and reading *Picture Post*. 'Nice work, that was. It's an ill wind that blows no one any good, and that's a fact. Nothing like a sense of impermanence to boost the holiday business. If you can't take it with you, you might as well enjoy yourse'n now. Bembows doubled their turnover during Korea.'

He didn't know that the boys had watched him dickering with his own devices in the Nissen hut only a few days previously, and Freddie wasn't going to tell him now. He looked much too dangerous with his little piggy eyes and his flushed red face.

'Don't you think it's a good thing, young 'un?'

He poked a finger into Freddie's ribs painfully, between the tables.

'Or are you one of they la-di-dah conchies?'

Freddie hadn't really thought about it much. He could remember the general joy of the war ending, and he knew that the atom bomb had been one of the things that helped it end. But a hydrogen bomb which could wipe out an entire country the size of Belgium . . .

'I suppose we have to have it if the other side have got it,' he said doubtfully.

'Course we do,' said Mr Leacock, 'stands to reason. Never get caught with your trousers down.'

It was a piece of advice that, metaphorically speaking, Mr Leacock had lamentably failed to heed himself, having been caught in his act – whatever it was – in the Nissen hut, but Freddie still didn't think it was worth drawing attention to the fact. Instead he went back to Belgium. One bomb would do for Belgium, and about five would do for Britain, but you'd need hundreds for a place the size of Russia. It seemed a bit unfair.

'Nice place they chose too,' continued Mr Leacock, 'for the test, si'thee. There's quite a nuance in that name. They didn't choose Devil's Island for it, did they? Oh no. They wanted an up-tempo name, something a bit optimistic. I expect they scoured the ocean for a suitably named atoll. And luke what they come up with. Monte Bello. Mount Beautiful. It's the kind of thing that gives you confidence in the authorities.'

Freddie wondered whether Mr Leacock had any moments of private doubt. Bembow, Bembow, did his mother know what a shit he was? But after all, thought Freddie, who was he to judge? The man was a pill, but his deeds were no worse than Freddie's thoughts, at least he wasn't a homo in love with his froggy guest.

This uncomfortable line of conjecture was interrupted by another conversational direction from Mr Leacock.

'Your friend down at the boatyard, thingummebob . . .'

'You mean Jackie?'

'That's right. Not quite all there, is he?'

'He's all right. He's good with the boats.'

'Not the point, lad. You're what we call a consumer. You're Joe Public. What the Bembows have to ask themselves is: does he match the platform?'

'You mean, the jetty?'

'It's all the rage in London, is platform. It's the stance, as you might say, the company posture.'

'Oh.'

'Now Jackie, posturely speaking, well, he's a bit like Frankenstein to be frank . . .'

'To be frank and stein.'

212

'Come again.'

'It doesn't matter.'

Aitken would have like the jest, but it went ricocheting past the top of Mr Leacock's left cortical hemisphere, probably because there was so much Brylcreem on top of it.

Bertrand excused himself and left the table, and Freddie was about to follow him when Mr Leacock said something that shook him to his foundations.

'Hold on, young 'un. Not so fast. How's the monster progressing?'

'M . . . monster?'

'Don't play silly buggers with me. The monster old Pa Seathwaite's doing for the Bembows. I gather you're giving him a hand.'

'Oh. You know about that?'

'Of course I know about that. I saw the publicity value as soon as Pa Seathwaite approached me. I commissioned it.'

'You're paying him money?'

'Well, we're not paying him dogshit. It's the Ettenwater Holiday Hamlet's logo, si'thee. We'll be announcing our plans at t'Regatta. I imagine you'll be there.'

'Oh. Yes,' said Freddie numbly. 'He didn't tell me.'

'Why should he tell you? You're just passing trade to him, like.'

'He should've told me.'

'He probably just thought, what the 'eck,' said Mr Leacock.

It wasn't that Freddie objected on principle to the Bembows' plans. He didn't even know what they were exactly. But he wouldn't have minded a few more things to do these holidays – the sort of things Bembows would doubtless provide next year – nice rubbishy food for a start – doughnuts, icecream, sausages and chips – and

213

what about cheap little motorboats – an amusement arcade – a coffee bar – a dance hall – a cinema – holiday girls with high hair and swirly skirts.

It was true he had become used to the silences and the emptiness of the place now. If there wasn't a real monster in the lake, he could believe that there might have been. He had climbed Stickletop and seen the trolls' heads sticking up in jagged rocky spikes on the way to the top, turned to stone by the sunrise. He had heard the wind in the Flute Stone, felt the fear in the mountain cave, watched the wild girls chasing cloud shadows on their ponies.

But it wasn't the betrayal of all this that hurt him so much. After all, he was only sixteen, it was grownups like his mother and Rollo who tut-tutted at the Vandalism of Progress, and who wouldn't have a television in the house because they were perfectly happy with whisky and bird-watching, who sent him off to these distant comfortless holidays, they would be the ones to frown on Bembows' Holiday Hamlets, not necessarily Freddie himself. He hadn't made his mind up yet.

No, what made him hurt and really angry was that Mr Seathwaite, for all his romantic eccentricity and his bear-ishness and St Sebastianism, didn't have the common politeness to tell him what he was really doing even though he was using his help – or the courage to admit that he was selling Great-Uncle Gussie's masterpiece for a handful of silver – because perhaps, worst of all, he thought that Freddie might have wanted a share of the spoils for himself.

'He probably thought,' said Mr Leacock aggressively as he got up from the table, 'it's none of thy damn business. Any road, there's nowt much you can do about it now.'

But there, thought Freddie as he watched him brush past the sauce table, making all the little relishes jitter and jump, there he must surely be wrong.

214

35

On the morning of the tenth day, the sun appeared in a cloudless sky, beaming across the water so that every ripple had its minnow of light.

It was a morning made for boating, and the boys set off early. But, as they approached the little shop, they saw a police car drive away.

There was no sign of Jackie in the boatyard. Come to think of it, there had been no sign of Isobel at Flat Foot breakfast.

'What was the police car doing? And where is Jackie?' Freddie asked the tiny old woman in the shop.

The old girl was in tears.

'They took Jack away. Someone reported him for mistrifying with that young lass.'

'She didn't report him, though.'

'She were nice to Jackie. She never reported him. It were someone else. They reckon she's sticking up for him because she's afraid of him. She dursn't tell the truth, they say. Afraid of Jackie? Whatever next? Well, I know what next. It'll be out of my shop, lock, stock and barrel, and it'll be Lakeland souvenirs and contraseptics before you can say Jack Robinson. T'place be in Jackie's name, d'ye see? That's why they want him out.'

'We'll see about this,' said Freddie.

Ever since he'd heard the news of Mr Seathwaite's perfidy, he had felt a righteous indignation welling up inside him. This was an internal pressure that he could more easily relieve than his resident frustration.

He turned on his heel and, with Bertrand padding after

him, went straight back to Flat Foot where Mr Leacock was last seen scraping up the remains of a black pudding.

Mrs Aylott, seeing them marching up the drive, stopped them in the hall.

'Yes,' she said, 'I would've told you but I didn't want to spoil your holidays. They've got Isobel for questioning. Poor Jackie. I didn't report him. I know I was vexed with her for pestering him, but I didn't mean him any harm. He sent me flowers. I had a talk with him. He wouldn't touch Isobel. She'd walk all over him. Anyone knows that.'

Freddie walked into the dining room. He felt like the Red Cross Knight. It was good to feel clean for a change. Mrs Aylott came in to watch.

Mr Leacock sat shovelling in toast and marmalade, and reading the day before yesterday's *Financial Times*.

'I believe you reported Jackie to the police,' he said.

Mr Leacock dropped his paper and looked up at Freddie with his dangerous piggy eyes.

'Yes, if it's any business of yours, snotty-nosed little parker. He were messing about with a minor, most regrettable. To say nothing of thieving flowers from t'churchyard.'

He helped himself to another piece of toast, spread it thickly with margarine and marmalade, and took a great bite. Freddie was mortified by his last remark. He'd actually suggested Jackie should go and pick them. They should've sent the police car for him.

'I'm glad Mr Aylott isn't here,' said Mrs Aylott. 'He doesn't take kindly to tell-tales.'

Mr Leacock worked his mouth like a guppy.

'I'll have you out of here on the dot, Missus. Don't expect any bounty. You'll have to go when you have to go.'

'That's if the sale goes through,' said Mrs Aylott.

'It has to go through,' said Mr Leacock, 'it's all signed and sealed. You try and pull out of it now and there'll be fireworks.'

'There were clauses,' said Mrs Aylott, 'that's all.'

'We know all about the clauses, Missus, and we all know about Mr Aylott's little problem.'

'Well, we *don't* all know about Mr Aylott's problem and I'd rather we didn't.'

'Suit yourse'n, Missus. I'll be off now, then. Don't think I'll forget this.'

'No, and we won't either,' said Freddie.

'You little . . .' said Mr Leacock, moving as if to strike him, but Mrs Aylott intervened.

'Not in my house,' she said. 'You can keep that sort of thing for Bembows.'

36

Freddie was waiting for the moment juste to tell Mrs
Seathwaite about the Leacock incident but she had
launched into metamorphosis over the lamb and spring
greens.

'Does one remember,' she said earnestly to Bertrand,
who was tucking into the roast potatoes like nobody's
business, 'from one's previous existence the moment
when the soul left the body? Does the karmic self recall
the instant it entered a new home? I sometimes think it
does. It is like . . .' She swayed incantatorily over the
polished mahogany, searching for a metaphor . . . 'It is
like being forcibly ejected from a familiar house . . .
wandering endlessly in a maze . . . in the dark . . . and at
long last seeing a distant light. We approach, conscious of
many a stirring and a rustling in the paths near us, here a
furtive footfall, there a beastly scamper, as others too see
what we have seen.'

She paused dramatically while Freddie peered at her
between forkfuls. No one talked like this at Marsh
Barton. Rollo would have laughed them out of court. He
even wondered whether she was having some sort of
private joke with them herself, but he had the boarding-
school's alertness to teasing, and he decided she was
genuinely potty about her subject like some of the masters
who seemed quite sane at other times. Her fine brow was
furrowed and her dark hair hung about her glasses like a
cloud before the sybil's cave.

'We press forward urgently,' she continued, 'jostling in
the path with many another shapeless shadow . . . until at

218

last we realize that we have turned the right corner just ahead of our rivals. We fling ourselves at the door. It opens . . . and we slam it shut. There is no one in the house. We see that it is as yet barely furnished. But it is full of light. It seems to be . . . in waiting. Sometimes, although we take up residence and fill the place with furniture, we feel it was never really meant for us. Only if we are lucky do we know for certain that it has been destined for us and us only since the beginning of time. Have you read the English writer J. B. Priestley, Bertrand?'

'No, I have not read.'

'He deals much with the question of time. Perhaps you have read Ouspensky? Or Gurdjieff?'

'I regret.'

'Time is the key, you see. It is not what we think it is, a one-way stream. No. Time has breadth as well as length. Time has height and depth. It has circumstances. And you, Bertrand, as you run with the wind in your hair, chasing a squirrel perhaps, as you did yesterday, do you not remember the former time, or is it lost forever in les halles . . .?'

She paused portentously before delivering the second half of her monumental phrase, but Bertrand got in first.

'I've been lost in Les Halles when I was little boy,' he confided.

But Mrs Seathwaite swept on regardless.

'Les Halles,' she intoned, 'des Morts.'

'Er,' said Freddie, and cleared his throat. It was obvious that Mrs Seathwaite had entirely forgotten his presence at the table. Thank goodness his momentary obsession with her had subsided. Her soft white thighs were flying, forgotten as a dream, but of course she couldn't be expected to know that.

'Yes, er Freddie.'

She swivelled her dark glasses at him, impatient of the interruption.

'Is it true,' he asked, 'that Mr Seathwaite's thinking of selling to the Bembows?'

No one had spelt it out in so many words but the truth, like a soul wandering in the dark, had suddenly come to him.

Mr Seathwaite, already guilty of gross deception, was planning to sell his birthright. His wife, though a mysterious creature, certainly cooked an excellent lunch, and it seemed a shame that she didn't know what was going on just because her attention was fixed on higher things.

Mrs Seathwaite's brow clouded and her dark glasses seemed to grow darker still.

'What d'you mean, Freddie? Spit it out,' she said.

He explained about Leacock and what he had learned of the Bembows' master plan. He told her about the proposed sale of Flat Foot. He told her about Great-Uncle Gussie's monster.

Mrs Seathwaite heard him out, asking judicious questions from time to time. Finally, as he reached the end of his report, she showed a most un-Platonic disgust.

'The devious insect,' she said. 'Mind you, I'd put nothing past him.'

'What are you going to do, Mrs Seathwaite?'

'I'm going to cook his goose. I know more of what goes on than he thinks. And if I can think of nothing else, I will scuttle the steam launch.'

'Ah non, not that,' cried Bertrand.

'For you, the boat shall be spared. You have interceded. But let us think. You say the Rural District Council is involved?'

'The Chairman is coming to the Regatta, that's what Mr Leacock said. He's going to announce permission to go ahead.'

'I know the Chairman of the Rural District Council. His sense of dignity is paramount – particularly if the press is involved. This is what we must do.'

She carefully enunciated a stratagem that was as masterly as it was simple. Freddie could not help but agree, though the thought of such a loss was painful.

'You are surprised perhaps, Freddie, that I can be such a dragon?'

'Yes,' he admitted, 'I am a bit, actually.'

'There is nothing more dangerous than the contemplative spirit when it is driven to action. Come, Bertrand. It is late for our walk.'

37

They arrived at the boathouse as the sun dipped, red as one of Shagger Davies's blind boils, behind the great collar of the western hills.

They found Mr Seathwaite giving *Proserpine* a polish for her appearance at the Regatta on Saturday. Before the operations on the monster, she had been removed from her berth and tied up at the visitors' jetty outside. Her tall funnel now swayed waggishly in the evening wavelets.

Mr Seathwaite was in a state of high good humour.

'It is working, youth. We have bubbles. There is a stirring in the depths. I shall make a small adjustment to the valve in case we are losing too much gas too soon. But the signs are good, youth. Come and see.'

He led them to the edge of the boathouse jetty.

At first there was nothing discernible in the muddy waters, only the reflection of the boathouse roof and the foreshortened shapes of their anxiously peering figures. Then, all at once, a great slow bubble, fat as a cowpat, welled up out of the depths and lazily burst at their feet.

'She breathes,' said Mr Seathwaite, with paternal pride.

A sudden stench of worse than death wafted across the quayside.

'Ooof,' said both boys in unison.

'You didn't expect violets, did you, youth?' he reproved the boys.

They watched and waited. There were other fat ghastly wellings, but no monster.

The minute hand on Mr Seathwaite's battered boat-house clock stole past nine. Five past . . . ten past . . . The surface of the water gave a little tremor as if in dread anticipation. A flurry of bubbles forced the boys back against the wall.

The air inside the boathouse was becoming foul, and both boys covered their faces with their handkerchiefs. Curiously, Mr Seathwaite himself seemed impervious to the malignity of the odours, drawing in great breaths and making learned comments on the life-cycle of the bacteria involved.

By a quarter past nine, however, even he was beginning to look mortified.

'We may have to get her up, youth. She's letting out too much air before she lifts.'

But once again there was a sudden trepidation in the water. The boys recoiled, preparing for the bursting pustules of bad wind, when Mr Seathwaite gave a great cry.

'THAR SHE BLOWS!'

They rushed forward again, hand on handkerchief.

It was the eye which showed first, a sullen glow almost indistinguishable from the reddish browny greys of the mud, but becoming brighter, flopping over, another eye showing, two prickly little ears, a snout, a muzzle, a turmoil of pouring water, a whole lopsided head held at an interrogatory angle, more bubbles, more turmoils, four streaming mud-green humps in diminishing order of size.

'HURRAH!' shouted Mr Seathwaite.

'BRAVO!' gasped the boys disregarding the foul miasma.

It really was the most impressive spectacle. Freddie, in spite of the implacable vexation he felt at Mr Seathwaite's shifty behaviour, could not help but join in the jubilation. This monster made the pocky little photographs of the

Loch Ness brigade look like an earthworm with rickets. This was a monster to be reckoned with, worthy of a thousand years of legend, Wordsworthy if it came to that. Pop this one up round the corner of the bay, and it'd give a poet something to write home about.

'Bring her to the side, youth, she needs more weight to starboard,' shouted Mr Seathwaite.

They hauled her in beside the jetty.

'I'll do the valve first,' said Mr Seathwaite. 'Hold her still, youth.'

He dived bravely under the monster's lolling jaw, and located the little opening.

'I'll give it a full turn,' said Mr Seathwaite, 'shut it off completely while we . . . Hold her still, youth . . .'

Freddie was craning to see what he was doing.

The monster burped right into Mr Seathwaite's face before he could shut it off, and even he turned a little pale.

'I'll be happy when she's in the water down at the south end opposite Church Meadow,' he said. 'Now, youth, bring me those weights by the window and I'll have her riding trim.'

Mr Seathwaite busied himself with the monster's midriff while Freddie held the creature up by its neck. It was a lengthy operation but finally it was done.

'Now youth and other youth,' said Mr Seathwaite, 'take her up tenderly and let's get her out in the open for the blow-out.'

They dragged her out to where *Proserpine* lay nodding in the twilight.

'I'll take the valve back now, youth. Half a turn, I think. Hold your nose if you're going to be finicky about it. And make sure you grab her or she'll sink.'

He plied the screw and, with a low moan, Ettie let out her hideous breath. She would indeed have dropped back into the water were it not for waiting hands which held her fast. The effluvium drifted out across the lake, making even the midges wilt.

'All aboard,' said Mr Seathwaite, 'keep that head and neck well down, youth. And other youth, keep that tail away from the screw.'

'Oui, mon capitaine,' said Bertrand.

They set off, with only the quietest of puffing from *Proserpine* to alert the casual watcher from the shore. Freddie kept the head well down near the waterline, one hand on jowl and other hand on neck.

Freddie would remember that strange journey for the rest of his life; the little launch with her own soft exhalations, the vapour making a fleeting canopy over their heads as the light breeze along the lake kept pace with their way; the trees on the shore shrouding in mist like candy-floss sticks; the flop and dopple of creatures over, in, or under the water; the layers of striated cloud making the last of the sunset seem not like a carbuncle now but a vast agate; in the distance the mountains smoking like volcanoes.

It was now ten o'clock and nearly dark.

Mr Seathwaite stopped *Proserpine*, monster-side away from the land, and they lay silently on the water looking at the gently rocking shoreline. Out of the corner of his eye, Freddie thought – just for an instant – that he saw a figure outlined above a low wall but it wasn't there when he looked again.

Already, they could see the preparations in hand for the Regatta. A small marquee had gone up, and a low stand had been erected for the speeches and awards.

'Nobody about,' said Mr Seathwaite. 'Look sharp now. When I say go, just lower her quietly into the water, and I'll run you straight to the jetty. Go!'

225

Ettie flung her head back, rolled over inertly, and was gone.

'Well done, youths,' said Mr Seathwaite as he delivered them to the quayside. 'I shall doubtless see you on Saturday. Don't look as if you're expecting anything.'

38

It was the afternoon before the Regatta, and Freddie was playing the Bechstein again. He was deflected from 'Bright the Vision that delighted', to the tune of Redhead, by a confused bellowing outside.

He cautiously opened the door to the hall and peeped out.

Mr Seathwaite, very red in the face, was berating his spouse.

'Where is the boy? I must have the boy.'

'The boy is mine,' Mrs Seathwaite was saying.

It reminded Freddie of Titania and Oberon squabbling in *A Midsummer Night's Dream*.

'I am dying, woman. I need the boy.'

'You are not dying. Would that you were. You have been dying of something or other ever since I've known you.'

'That is the effect of life.'

'The boy is not for you.'

Freddie saw Bertrand poised on the stairs, watching the proceedings. He suddenly knew that Bertrand and Mrs Seathwaite had been deceiving him – worse, making fun of him with all that stupid dog story.

'What are you dying of, I should like to know,' Mrs Seathwaite continued.

'I have cancer.'

'Cancer? Cancer where?'

'Cancer in my heart.'

'You do not get cancer in the heart.'

'I do.'

'Eat your heart out, then. You should not have allowed Jojo to drown.'

'Ah. Now. Now we have it. I should feel guilty, I suppose. Who was the one having an affair, soiling your wedding sheets?'

'Do not speak so loud. You have been drinking. Go back immediately before the boy sees you.'

Even in the midst of his astonishment, Freddie was hurt by the fact that she was only referring to one boy, one boy who seemed to matter, and he knew it wasn't him.

At this point, Bertrand started coming down the stairs. Mr and Mrs Seathwaite turned to watch him. Mrs Seathwaite was evidently in some anxiety that he had heard the whole conversation. Without speaking, he went up to Mr Seathwaite and took him by the hand.

'Viens,' he said.

'See,' said Mr Seathwaite, tottering, 'see which one he prefers.'

'Please,' said Bertrand, 'please calm yourself. Let us walk down to the lake calmly.'

'I shall destroy you,' said Mrs Seathwaite to her husband.

'Too late,' he said as he lurched down the drive supported by the French boy.

Mrs Seathwaite now turned and saw Freddie framed in the doorway.

'I'm sorry,' she said, collecting herself, 'my nieces always refer to a French friend I had in the war, Free French, you know . . .'

'Ah,' said Freddie.

'It is a rather cruel family joke, typical of the Seathwaites, and of course, my husband. They refer to him as the French poodle. He was in love with me, er Freddie. That is the plain truth of it. My niece told me that you had asked about the stone. J. S. was Jean-Jacques de

228

Selincourt. He was drowned, or drowned himself, in the lake here. He was very depressed. His country had fallen, he himself had been quite badly wounded. His brother had been killed by the Gestapo, his young wife had simply disappeared. He was in love with me, but I was married. My husband was here, working down at the boathouse on an Admiralty project – you know he was involved with underwater acoustics – he should have seen Jean in the water but unaccountably or, as I sometimes think deliberately, did not. I am trying to explain to you, Freddie, the reason for our deception. My interest in reincarnation was, of course, no deceit.'

'Oh,' said Freddie, unhelpfully, a cold toad in his heart.

'Jean wore that costume Bertrand found in the attic, a fancy dress party we had. It was then my husband gave him the nickname, Jojo. He said it was a dog's costume. Bertrand looked so like him, you see. Oh, he is younger, of course but . . . He will leave in three days, Freddie, and go south with you. I will not see him again. There is no one here. My husband naturally wishes to spoil my happiness. He says he loves the boy. Perhaps he was in love with Jean. I have known, you see, of my husband's preference since our honeymoon. Bertrand seems to have the gift of pacifying him. They do not . . . do anything. I am sure of that. Go down now, please, Freddie, and bring him back.'

Freddie had retreated before the force of her story and indeed of the passions she was revealing, into the drawing room. He found himself sitting on the arm of one of the big chairs while she stood over him. The living exposure of passions which he had only read about before was almost as shocking as the bare-faced deceit of the woman. He did not know what to do, where to look. All he wanted to do really was to hare back to his bedroom in Flat Foot, draw the curtains, and be alone.

The thought of Bertrand's duplicity compounded with Mrs Seathwaite's lies – for whatever reason she had told them – was bitter to him. They must all have been laughing at him, even the nieces.

However, he had to know if the deception was complete.

Mumbling miserably to Mrs Seathwaite, he ran out of the house and down the familiar path towards the lake.

Arriving at the boathouse, he paused, crouching under the eaves out of the rain. Did he really want to know if Bertrand was being unfaithful with Mr Seathwaite too? Wasn't infidelity in thought and word enough? Did he need to witness the deed to know the monstrous nature of the crime against him?

He lifted his head to the window and looked in.

Bertrand was sitting in the bed cradling Mr Seathwaite's head with an expression of the greatest sorrow and tenderness. It was enough for Freddie.

He turned and ran back in the rain to the bleak little guesthouse. The truth was, he saw it quite clearly, that all this time Bertrand had really been a homo and he hadn't wanted Freddie. That was the fact of the matter. That was all there was to it. Pretty bloody depressing when you came to think about it.

39

When Bertrand finally arrived back, it was nine o'clock, and he was miles too late for any food, but Freddie had warned Mrs Aylott, and there were no scenes.

Over his solitary sardines, Freddie had resolved to say nothing of the afternoon's activities, and on Bertrand's return he maintained a stubborn air of indifference.

In the Res Lounge, Bertrand hovered, seeming to want to talk, and when he offered to teach Freddie poker, he agreed with cool politeness. Somehow a full pack of cards had been located.

With the wireless tuned to its only available station, the intermittent strains of 'O mein Papa' actually increased the sensation of isolation, as though they were drifting further and further from the golden trumpety centre of things.

Freddie was just beginning to get the hang of the game, and feeling rather grown up about it, even though he had no intention of admitting any such thing to Bertrand, when there was an almighty clap of thunder and all the lights went out, along with the fractured larynx of Lita Roza who had taken over from Eddie Calvert.

'Zut alors,' said Bertrand. 'J'aime pas le tonnerre.'

Freddie shrugged in the dark. Curiously enough his endemic nervousness did not extend to thunderstorms. Even so, he was impressed by the vigour of the tempest that now unfolded. It was as though the elements were themselves playing out some of the passions of the day, a phenomenon which Gibbers Thompson had pointed out on more than one occasion in Shakespeare.

Eventually a light could be discerned approaching. It proved to be carried by Mrs Aylott.

'That's the electricity gone for the night,' she told them. 'Here comes a candle to light you to bed.'

In the bedroom, Bertrand shivered like an oeuf en gelée while the storm biffed and banged around the lake. All it needed was Handel's Firework Music, which Freddie would gladly have supplied if Flat Foot had sported an upright. He gazed out at the celestial mayhem for some time, hoping that a flash would illuminate a monster or stone giant playing ducks and drakes with a thunderbolt, but he could see no break in the ruffled shiny contour of the water. The only monster was here, inside.

Freddie blew out the candle, and they climbed into their beds.

It was one of those storms that play havoc with the timorous by seeming to depart and then pouncing back again.

In spite of the turmoil in the heavens, the sound of the rain outside had its usual soothing effect. Freddie was almost asleep when he felt the bedclothes being lifted and Bertrand inserting himself between the sheets.

Neither of them said anything. Bertrand lay and shivered.

At last Freddie felt Bertrand begin to touch him. He almost let it happen. But the injustice was too great to lie down with.

'Infidèle,' said Freddie, drawing on reserves of Racine, and detaching the tempting hand. He climbed out of bed. Bertrand made no attempt to follow him.

Freddie spent the rest of the night in Bertrand's bed, alone.

He woke to the rare sensation of warmth. A strip of hot sunshine was lying across his face. He looked across at Bertrand, still asleep, and drew the curtains.

The storm had cleared the clouds and a brilliant light bounded into the room, stirring even the French boy from his sloth.

'Oof,' said Bertrand, wincing.

The extraordinary thing was, thought Freddie, the boy seemed to have no sense of shame about yesterday at all. You could tell by the way he went about the wash-basin that he was treating this morning like a perfectly standard one.

Freddie couldn't understand it at all. Sex and shame were indivisible. It was the accepted thing. Every precept, every lecture had dinned into Freddie and his schoolfellows the dangers both moral and physical that stemmed from abuse of their bodies.

Later, he would discover the same acceptance of sex as an act – like eating – among girls. They had a good meal or a bad meal or even a poisonous meal, but they didn't feel guilty about it – unless of course they were slimming, but that was something else.

This guilt thing seemed to be a speciality of or for English boarding-school boys. It was the first time that Freddie had been made aware of it – and of course on this occasion he thought it was Bertrand who was the odd one. Here the boy was, sleeping with practically everyone in sight, and he seemed to have no guilt about it at all. It made him angry, and he was brusque with Bertrand's request for dentifrice.

'Why are you crossed?' asked Bertrand as they walked down the corridor to breakfast. 'Do you not like to make love with me?'

'Shh,' said Freddie, blushing furiously. 'Not now.'

'I do not like to make love now.'

'Will you stop talking about making love? Making love is what you do with a girl.'

'Alors, what do you call it, then?'

233

'Well,' said Freddie, making circling motions with his hand and helping himself with the other to cornflakes.

Mutual Masturbasssshion hardly seemed to do the subject justice.

Bertrand started talking about the Seathwaites. This was something Freddie had been dreading.'

'I am sorry, Freddie, that I did not tell you earlier but it would only have made you angry. Better to be angry for three days than for eight. They are very interesting for me, those two. I am sorry for them.'

'What about me?' asked Freddie.

It was one of his favourite cries at home. What about me, what about me?

'I am not sorry for you, Freddie. I am sorry that you felt love for me. But you do not want to make love.'

'Shh. No. No,' cried Freddie, wildly.

Isobel might come in at any moment.

'Anyway, it would not be very nice for your mother.'

'Leave my mother out of it,' cried Freddie.

'Someone was drowned in the lake. Perhaps he was let to drown. Perhaps he was killed. Mr Seathwaite thinks the body is going to come back. He only has to find it. It will resolve the question. Mrs Seathwaite does not want this. You know what I believe. I believe there is no body.'

Freddie all at once felt better about Bertrand. The fact that he could have gone to bed with him suddenly meant that he wasn't so sure he wanted to. That relaxed French attitude was a passion-killer and no mistake. He felt something, an oppression lifting from him. Could it be possible? He was free?

Yes, he thought, perhaps I really am. Then why don't I feel entirely happy about it? Silly, really. English guilt has something to be said for it. It is like our taste for curry. Perhaps love would be a pale meal without it. Why was life so contradictory?

A preoccupied-looking Isobel entered bearing two plates of thin grey sausages. She gave a sigh and retired without speaking.

The sausages lay there, begging to be lashed with guilt.

'Eat up, Bertrand,' said Freddie. 'You will need your strength for our tennis match today.'

'Tennis match. What tennis match?'

'Today we have to play the girls.'

40

The encounter proved to be a fiasco. Freddie had feared as much and had hoped to escape the engagement, but Diana, the younger one, had insisted, saying they were hacking off to Ulpha tomorrow and wouldn't be back until the boys had gone, so it was their last chance to thrash them.

She hadn't mentioned who was to thrash whom, but it was clear to Freddie that she intended to be in the thrasher's seat.

Elizabeth was very good and Diana would have been brilliant if she hadn't tended too much towards the erratic. As it was, they trounced the boys 6–2, 6–2. Freddie's serve, always a vulnerable area, let him down completely, but the real trouble was Bertrand, who seemed completely listless.

After the match was over and the warm-handled rackets were back in their presses, Bertrand made some excuse and wandered off towards the house. Elizabeth went back with him to change, and Freddie was left with Diana. It was hell being beaten by girls.

'Bloody awful tennis you play,' she said, 'it's worse than your riding if such a thing were possible.'

'I think the court takes a bit of getting used to,' he replied, nettled.

It was true, the ancient En Tout Cas had deteriorated to the point of disintegration in places.

'You know what they say about bad workmen and their tools,' she said, swinging one pink leg over the other. 'Like to come and see the secret passage?'

'What's that?'

'It goes from the cellars up to one of the bedrooms. It was supposed to have been built by Mad Jack Seathwaite so he could sneak up to seduce a cousin.'

'Oh,' said Freddie. 'Right.'

'We'd better bring a coat and a torch. It's cold down there, and dark as hell inside.'

They walked back to the house, Freddie casting stolen glances at her strong pink shanks and the waggle of her bottom in the tennis dress.

She left him in the hall while she went off for a torch, and he inspected the disapproving faces of the Seathwaites past, trying to locate Mad Jack who didn't have any right to disapprove of anything.

She returned with a couple of coats and a bicycle lamp.

'This way,' she said. 'Bowels of the earth.'

Freddie was fond of cellars. There was something mysterious, romantic, about the undergroundness of them – the mustiness, the cobwebby corners, the obscure unwanted things that collected in them. They were the subterranean complement of attics.

Attics, however, didn't have bottles, and these were the true glory of the place. Not the empty Gordons and Haigs, or the tonics and the ginger ales, but the serious magical forms: ancient limbecks, mystic carboys and pipkins, and the immemorial soda siphons in their chain mail. These were the temples of mystery. And then, of course, there was the wine.

Wine played a very small part in the life of Barton Manor Farm. Freddie's mother drank very little, preferring her own home-made country wines when she did; Rollo stuck almost exclusively to sherry and spirits; so genuine French wine was a rarity in the house – something extravagant and desirable to be approached with sibylline reverence as much as Dionysiac delight.

The Hell Hall cellars were no disappointment. The bottles by no means filled the generous rackage but they made a good show. Freddie paused to inspect the array.

There were clarets and burgundies, high-necked bottles from Alsace, brown and green-glassed succulences from the Rhine and the Mosel. There was champagne, and Madeira, and ancient dusty crusty bottles of port. Freddie would have lingered but it was not to be.

'Come on,' said Diana. 'It's hell's cold in a tennis skirt. Hold the torch while I open the door.'

She led the way to a small portal at the furthest cobwebbiest end of the cellars. The key turned, the door creaked, and Freddie found himself at the bottom of a low dim curved-roof stairway, fusty-smelling and sinister, well, dexter actually, because it wound up to the right.

Diana led the way. As the door closed behind them, Freddie experienced a surge of apprehension. What if they were locked in? But he could hardly babble like a weed with Diana and her pink pins striding so purposefully up the stairs in front of him.

After about fifty steps, the stairway ended in a flat passage with a door at the far end. Diana extracted a key from her coat and opened it. Daylight poured in from some unseen window. He was about to step out when Diana shut the door in his face.

'Not so fast,' she said. 'I thought you wanted to see the secret passage.'

'I did,' said Freddie. 'This is it, isn't it?'

'No,' said Diana, taking his hand and placing it under her tennis skirt. 'This is it.'

'Oh gosh,' said Freddie.

Diana's tennis knickers felt very secret indeed. Freddie was overcome with a mixture of emotions. Part of him was elated by this sudden and unexpected fulfilment of so many adolescent reveries, but other parts were appalled

238

at the proximity of a pleasure so long deferred. Would he be able to do it? And what about Bertrand? Could he be unfaithful to the faithless French boy just out of curiosity?

Diana had no such qualms.

'Lie down on the coat,' she ordered. 'You can feel my chest if you like.'

Diana's bosoms weren't at all what he had been led to expect by *Health and Efficiency*. He had thought that bosoms were hard and firm like balloons; but Diana's as she lay back on the coat were all over the place, like runny Camembert.

He stroked them manfully, noticing that his erection had gone pathetically limp. She took his other hand and stuck it once more between her legs.

'Go on,' she said.

He didn't know quite what she meant. Doubtless when she undressed some more, as it seemed was her general plan, nature would take over. One sight of her nakedness would inflame him to the point of mindlessness.

Meanwhile his hand at least obeyed the will of its master. He rubbed it up and down the Bri-Nylon wondering whether it was having any effect whatsoever on his fair equestrian. The material felt soft and warm, but Diana gave no sign of satisfaction.

Suddenly she leant over and grasped his tool in rein-roughened hands and rubbed it as if she were putting soap on a particularly dingy saddle.

'Now,' she said. 'I hope you've got a French letter handy.'

As a matter of fact, he did have one. Rather old and squashed, it was one of the things that Aitken said no self-respecting chap should be without.

He nodded at her enquiry. With a sudden expert movement, she lifted her dress and took off her knickers.

'There,' she said. 'Now stick it in.'

This was the moment that Freddie, and the whole of the Fifth Form, had been waiting for. This would show Bertrand. He stole a look at the vision that would drive all rational thought from his mind. He saw a white belly, a triangular tangle of pubic hair, and a menacing little crevice in the middle of it.

His tool, rubbed roughly into half-life, dropped like a plummeting goshawk.

'Oh do hurry up,' said Diana. 'I've got to go and exercise Major.'

'I . . . I'm sorry,' muttered Freddie, knowing the thing was impossible.

'Elizabeth bet me you were a homo. You're not, are you?'

He glanced at the door which Diana had omitted to lock. Perhaps it was in every sense a way out.

'I think there's someone coming,' he said.

'Well, one thing's for sure,' said Diana. 'It certainly isn't me.'

He looked down, crestfallen, and saw a piece of paper in the torchlight. Stooping to retrieve it – he thought it might have come from his own pocket – he found it was a note in French on a piece of folded paper, addressed to the French boy.

'Have you been here with Bertrand? he asked Diana, shocked.

'Don't be a weed. Let me look.'

She took the note and examined it.

'It's Aunt's writing. It's a French letter from Aunt Elspeth.'

So the secret passage was a popular haunt.

'I can't make out what it says,' said Diana. 'They teach us French at school but they don't teach us to understand it.'

'Could I have it back, please?

'It's not yours.'

'Give it back.'

Freddie could feel the blush of anger, stoked by humiliation, spreading across his face.

'Temper, temper. Pinched your boyfriend, has she? Little homo.'

'I'm not. I . . .'

'Oh forget it.'

Freddie watched her stalk out onto the landing, the strong bottom twitching the tennis skirt once more, pink legs pumping the carpet, eager to be away from such a worm.

So. He was a failure as a ladies' man as well as a dud queer . . .

What had Mr Seathwaite called him? A snivelling little tosser?

Maybe that was all he was. Perhaps it really did send you mad.

He unfolded Mrs Seathwaite's French letter.

'When you've finished stuffing your face with strawberries, I have something for you to do in the gazebo,' he read.

Apart from the roguish intimacy of the first phrase, the French pun on 'à faire' and 'affaire' was not lost on Freddie. Something very like it was used to good effect in Charles Dibdin's song 'The Jolly Young Waterman' which he'd carolled to Bertrand only a few days before:

'And he eyed the young rogues with so charming an air
That this waterman ne'er was in need of a fare.'

The inference was unmistakable. The 'to do' had been going on right under his nose. For all Mrs Seathwaite's soulful expostulations and spiritual talk, she was no better than those masters who were ace at their subjects but whose chief interest seemed to be putting a hand on your knee. Only she hadn't just been putting a hand on his knee, she'd been letting him – what was Diana's musical phrase? – stick it in her.

He didn't mind now as far as Bertrand went. It was just that it made him, Freddie, look such a fool.

41

Regatta Day dawned bright and blue, which was against all expectation.

Freddie occupied the morning in packing, walking by the lake in the sun, and feeling increasingly uneasy. Mrs Seathwaite had after all, he thought, deceived him equally in her way, and so had Bertrand, twice. Why should Mr Seathwaite be singled out?

However, the thing had been done and there was no way of undoing it. Mrs Seathwaite had said it would be a blow struck for the preservation of the countryside, but Freddie thought it might be more like a stab in the back.

By twelve he was back at Flat Foot wishing the Regatta could happen this afternoon instead of this evening, and he could get the thing over with.

Bertrand had gone off to Hell Hall for lunch, and Freddie couldn't bring himself to go over and join them for all the roast chicken in Cumberland. So he took his packed lunch and a History of English Literature up the path towards the Mad Monk's crying-ground. Seating himself on a smooth boulder, with the lake sparkling below him, he tried to concentrate on his textbook. Sometimes histories like this helped by giving more of a general picture. He needed a whole bloody mural with Wordsworth.

'Wordsworth, though undeniably a great poet, has often been one of the most difficult to approach. The self-conscious diction, the didactic intent, all too frequently obscure a freshness of perception and a genuine response to nature,' he read.

What did it all mean? What was a genuine response to nature? He had had the opportunity of a genuine response to nature with Diana and he had signally failed to respond. He shut his eyes and tried to have a genuine response to nature.

He concentrated on sensing the warmth of the sun, the softness of the breeze, the distant bleat of a lamb.

It was strange. They had been pleasant enough when they had crept in unmindfully at the corner of his eye, but the more he thought about them and tried to have a genuine response, the less response he seemed to feel.

Perhaps it was like happiness, you only knew you were happy after the event. A phrase came to his mind from other Wordsworth reading: 'Emotion recollected in tranquillity.'

Suddenly he understood what the old boy was on about.

What you felt was important, not what you thought you should feel. And if you felt you didn't want to stick it in Diana, then you were right. And if you stopped thinking about it so much anyway, you probably enjoyed it more when it happened. And if it didn't happen, you didn't miss what you weren't thinking about.

He stayed up on the hill for some time, eating Spam sandwiches, and thinking, and not thinking.

The glitter of something moving beside the southern end of the lake, between the tents, caught his eye. He looked more closely. It was a silver band. He inspected his watch. It was five o'clock. He had said he would meet Mr Seathwaite at six.

42

The field was full of folk.

English fêtes, of course, normally occur in the mid-afternoon, but the Ettenwater Regatta traditionally ended with fireworks, so it was not declared open until five.

By now, as Freddie walked with Mr Seathwaite, the event was in full swing. They passed sideshows of various kinds – hoop-la, bric-à-brac, jumble, darts, buried treasure, guess the weight of the cake, lucky dip – and moved on to where judging was in progress for the various classes of produce.

It was strange to see such a normally sequestered spot so crowded.

'Oh yes,' said Mr Seathwaite as they strolled among the throng, 'I can see many changes when the Bembows come. There will be music everywhere.'

He flung his arms wide to embrace the echoing cliffs and summits.

A man who was trying to bowl for a pig at one of the side-stalls looked up in irritation. His throw had been seriously put out by the exuberance of Mr Seathwaite's gesture.

'I say, old man, do you mind frightfullah?' said the man, in a stupidly offensive voice.

Mr Seathwaite looked at him thoughtfully.

'You don't need a pig,' he said at length. 'Your wife wouldn't know which one to talk to.'

Mr Seathwaite walked on oblivious of the stream of invective this provoked. He was too worked up over the

245

approach of the great materialization to be sidetracked by mundanities. He continued to amplify his vision.

'The lake will be partially heated,' he went on. 'A large plexiglass structure will entirely cover this southern end. There will be dodgem boats, and all manner of water sports. A maintenance man will have full-time employment dredging out the testimony of summer nights. The monster will manifest every evening at twilight. And Druids will ritually sacrifice a maiden every Sunday before dinner. Hell Hall, which might be too menacing a name for the mums and dads and Kennies and Dawns, Hell Hall will be rechristened Liberty Hall. Follow your inclination will be the keynote. Do what you will. I see it coming. The forecast of the Beast. Don't just covet your neighbour's wife. Fornicate with her until her false teeth rattle as she knocks back the champagne perry!'

'Won't it be rather a shame, spoiling Hell Hall and the lake?' asked Freddie.

'Not a bit of it. Hell has changed. Hell Hall's hellishness has grown out of date. You clearly have not been following contemporary authority. Desolate, dangerous, moody Hell is out. It has changed to a comfortable grey, or beige. A holiday camp is exactly the right location for Hell. Or shall we say that Hell is exactly the right location for a holiday camp? Ha. Besides it will mortify my wife.'

They had reached a point on the grass near the Regatta's prize-giving podium. Various cups had already been awarded for home produce and aquatic egg and spoon races, and people were already crowding the shore for the results of the long-distance sculls.

There was no sign of Mrs Seathwaite or Bertrand, but Mr Seathwaite seemed to have forgotten the boy for the moment. The misery-me introspection, the whiskyfied rancour, were gone, and in their place was something almost like optimism in a black sort of way.

Freddie felt emboldened to ask a question that had been bothering him.

'Why do you hate the lake?'

Mr Seathwaite stopped and looked at him with a bright and beady eye. Had he gone too far after all?

'Who says I hate the lake?'

'You always seem to call it bloody lake. You say it's hellish.'

'You are right, youth. I do. It is a bloody lake. If I could give the word and start that scree falling, I would do it like a shot. Fill the whole thing in. That lake has sat winking and bubbling evilly at my door throughout my life. It is my first memory. It was always ripe for mischief. Two little Seathwaite girls drowned in it in 1685. A cousin went in 1759. Mad Jack Seathwaite got blind drunk and tried to swim it on his favourite mare. They both went down. I believe I was conceived on its banks in a mad moment of Edwardian devil-may-care. And he did care, it seems, for look at this fruit of those distant loins. A sere fruit, youth, begotten for mischance.'

'I see,' said Freddie, uncomprehendingly.

'I doubt if you do. There comes a moment in life – you will find it, youth, for I perceive the seeds of melancholy in you – when you suddenly realize that your future has become fatally entangled in your past. It cannot extend any further. Some writer chappie said somewhere that writing's like a Houdini act. You get yourself in a hell of a knot, then as if by magic you wriggle out of it. Life is like that, youth, not just novels. And sometimes you just can't undo the knot. Hullo, fire engine.'

Freddie turned and saw a distant flash of tinkling red going down the How road.

'Forest fire, I expect. Don't suppose it's Hell Hall going up. That would be a stroke of luck. I wouldn't need to

247

sell to Bembows then. Although, come to think of it, I'd do it all the same.'

'Where will you go?'

'Oh anywhere. As long as I don't have to live near her. All I ever needed was some cash.'

'What will you do then?'

'Mope.'

'What about Mrs Seathwaite?'

'Mrs Seathwaite can go to Hell. As a matter of fact, she never left.'

'What about J. S.? You'll have to give up the search. Bertrand says he wonders if he ever existed.'

'Bertrand is impertinent. The man drowned. I saw him go. The water was too cold. Perhaps I could have rescued him. But he had not behaved well. Mrs Seathwaite said I had killed him. It has been a slur. I determined to fish him out and lay his unbroken skull at her door. Remember that strong echo, youth. I went back yesterday and found bones.'

'Bones? A skeleton?'

Freddie thought that Mr Seathwaite must not only be mad but must think him mad too.

'Surely skeletons don't float?'

'The lake gives up her own.'

'Is that true?'

'"On a huge hill, cragged and steep, Truth stands, and he who will reach her, about must and about must go,"' said Mr Seathwaite.

The silver band launched into a suite from Handel's Water Music.

'The second cornet is atrocious,' said Mr Seathwaite. 'I also used to play in the school band. That same school where I learned Laughing and Grief.'

Not much of the former, thought Freddie. Still, seeing him so mellow now, he was beginning to feel horribly guilty. He wished again that he could unmake what he had done. But it was too late now.

'Hullo. Another engine. Must be quite a blaze. They'll fry, poor buggers.'

The declining sun was still doing its best to make up for the deficiencies of the last fortnight, and the evening was still ridiculously warm. Freddie sweltered in his Aertex shirt and denim shorts, and Mr Seathwaite in his ancient blazer, yellowed whites and yellowed striped tie looked deliquescent.

It was now seven o'clock. There was still no sign of Bertrand or Mrs Seathwaite.

A gun sounded, and a race of tiny sailing boats was under way. Bets were already being taken by a bookie from Whitehaven for the next race – a rowing event.

An indecipherable voice was issuing a list of something over the loudspeakers, and the silver band lurched into the Posthorn Gallop.

Every now and then someone would stop and say hullo to Mr Seathwaite. And, perhaps more frequently, Freddie would notice others who would make a sudden dash out of the way in order to avoid the meeting.

To either eventuality, Mr Seathwaite seemed oblivious. He was anticipating an apotheosis.

The approach of the great moment was affecting Freddie very differently. This, coupled with the intimations of his return home tomorrow, left him in a heightened and increasingly nervous frame of mind. As he moved through the crowd, he began to experience a strange combination of loneliness and reluctance to be gone from here. He couldn't conceive of real life going on anywhere else. Bedfordshire would seem flat, in every sense, beside it. He had passed through something and could never return. His mother, Rollo, Hildegard the au pair, the whole

Marsh Barton ménage, would no longer be home but a lodging between visits.

And yet where would home be? Where was home?

Here, surrounded by the strange rites of an English summer, he felt his childhood drop off like a snakeskin.

Wordsworth wouldn't have approved. He felt childhood was just the job. But then Wordsworth didn't have to eat greasy bacon with eyes in it, go to pony club dances, and be teased by Rollo. William Wordsworth? W. W.? Rollo would've probably called him WeeWee.

'Come on, dearie. Read yer fortune. Only two bob a go.'

He gesticulated at Mr Seathwaite, who had stopped to talk to a Rural Dean (the man had tried to sidestep but too late), and entered the booth where the gypsy was settling herself behind her crystal ball.

'Let me take your hand, dearie. Oh yes, I see a fair lady coming your way. You know a fair lady? Well, you will do. You haven't been happy, have you? Not to worry. Only fools is happy in this world. Look out for the fire that never dies. I suppose we all should. I see a snake. That's for deception. Riches? Oh you will make money, but you know what they say about money, don't you, dearie? Your cross is dissatisfaction. Let me look at my ball. I see a car. Yes, you are going on a journey, a lady and gentleman. I see other cars . . . black . . . That is sufficient. Cross me palm with silver, dearie. It don't buy happiness but it do pay the dos. Get me a cheese roll, Billy. Next!'

He emerged to see Mr Seathwaite sloping off to the bar with a reprobate in a baggy suit who looked like an ex-vicar. Knowing that it would at least be a sure place to find him when the moment came, he circulated once more around the arena.

He brought an icecream, ate half, and threw it away.

He saw Leacock shepherding a middle-aged couple into a tent placarded with lettering that said: BEMBOWS – GROWING LIKE FUN!

He saw another little marquee, sandwiched between the WVS and St John's Ambulance, which said: MEET YOUR RURAL DISTRICT COUNCIL. It was empty.

Finally he met Mrs Aylott, who was buying a cake at the Home Produce stand. He had always suspected that she had a perverse instinct for the unpalatable, and even before greeting her he could see at a distance that she was carefully selecting the driest sponge from a mouth-watering selection of moist-looking delicacies.

'Hullo, Mrs Aylott,' he said dully.

She turned and smiled at him. She was wearing a rather pretty printed blue shirt-waist dress, and her hair – normally done up in a straggly bun – was hanging in loose curls about her shoulders. She had taken off her glasses.

She looked about fifteen years younger than the forty he had assigned to her. The change heartened him. He noticed that she had bosoms.

'You look nice,' he said, trying not to look at her chest.

'Why thank you, Freddie. I may call you Freddie?'

'Of course.'

'I was buying a cake for your supper. Do you like the look of it?'

'Well.'

He didn't want to be rude.

'I think that one might be more fun.'

He pointed to a juicy-looking fruit cake.

'You're probably right,' she sighed. 'Mr Aylott always gives me stick if I get anything too nice. It goes too quickly. Still, don't suppose it matters if we're selling up to Bembows.'

She exchanged the cake, and Freddie walked beside her as she moved on to the next stall.

'Where is Mr Aylott?' he asked politely, not that he had much time for him.

'He had to stay in Whitehaven. It was the only day his accountant could see him, and someone had to take Isobel into the police station again. They'll be staying with his folks tonight. They live there, you know. Isobel was that sick at missing the Regatta, but I told her, Jackie's got to have someone stand by him.'

'I feel sort of responsible. Those flowers . . .'

'It's not you, it's Leacock, isn't it? Anyway, I said to the police that she'll go and tell them exactly what's what. She was just fooling around with them the first time. She hates the cops, as she calls them. Leacock tried to bribe her, of course. Typical her. She took the chewing gum and Hershey Bars – where does he get Hershey Bars? – and told him she was going to shoot her mouth off all the same.'

'I wish there was something I could do.'

'You're a good sort, Freddie.'

She nearly said boy but changed it to sort just in time. Freddie was grateful, and smiled at her.

'Maybe there will be something,' she said. 'Who knows?'

Freddie looked at his watch. He could feel the minutes whizzing past like water before a weir. There was only half an hour to go before the monster was due to manifest.

'I'd better go,' he said. 'I promised to meet Mr Seathwaite. See you later.'

'Oh, I nearly forgot. Your mother rang. She asked me to say they'd be arriving tomorrow about midday. She asked if everything was all right. I said I thought it was. It has been all right, hasn't it? I said the French boy was all right too. I said he seems all right. That was right, wasn't it? Good.'

'Yes, yes.'

'Where is he anyway?'

'Up at Hell Hall.'

'What a pity. He's missing all the fun.'

'Everything's all right,' said Freddie. 'I'd better go.'

He found Mr Seathwaite sure enough in the bar, surrounded by empty whisky glasses. He was in high good humour.

'Ah, youth. A stoup of ale for the youth.'

'No, thank you,'said Freddie.

He wanted to keep a clear head.

There was a roll on the drums outside. Freddie led Mr Seathwaite back to the water's edge. The prize-giving was over. A buzz of excitement indicated that the crowd sensed firework time. A new voice spoke over the loudspeakers.

'This year's Ettenwater Regatta . . .' loud cheers . . .'Firework Display . . .' prolonged cheers . . .'comes to you, ladies and gentlemen, by courtesy of Bembows Holiday Hamlets . . .' roars of applause . . .'It is no secret that Bembows are taking a monster interest'. . . laughter, guffaws, wolf whistles . . .'in Ettenwater just now. By this time next year, given the approval of our friends on the Council who, I believe I'm right in saying, have not been unsympathetic . . .' yer yer yer . . .'we could well be celebrating the opening of Bembows Ettenwater and all that that entails in terms of local employment, trade and prosperity . . .' crescendos of enthusiasm and jocundity . . .'Yes, ladies and gentlemen, Bembows are going to put Ettenwater, from being something of a backwater, to something that is well and truly on the map.'

The approbation which greeted this last impertinence was like a force of nature itself. Freddie feared for the stability of the scree.

There was something familiar about the tones of the speaker, mutilated by the equipment though they were.

'It's Leacock,' he said to Mr Seathwaite.

'Who?'

'Leacock.'

'What?'

'Leacock.'

'Go and have a piss, then,' replied Mr Seathwaite.

'Shhhhh,' said an angry voice to murmurs of assent.

Freddie thought he recognized the pig-bowler.

They were all listening enraptured to the glorious things that Bembows were going to do-io for them.

Freddie now spotted a prosperous-looking couple – whom he guessed to be the Bembows themselves – moving onto the podium by the water's edge, along with the local dignitaries and the Mayor of somewhere.

The fireworks began.

As it turned out, they were the most elaborate pyrotechnics the Ettenwaterers and their neighbours had seen since VE day. Some said they even excelled them.

There were rockets and flying squibs and wonderful Roman candles that changed colour and spat fire; there were bangers and thumpers and whizzers and whooshers.

The band started playing something that dimly resembled Handel's Firework Music.

The whole event provided a spectacle that would normally have afforded Freddie the utmost amusement; but dread was growing in him, finding out the cracks in his centre like mycelium in a piece of old cheddar. He was in a blue funk at the end when Leacock's voice announced the set piece, the piece of resistance, he said, which symbolized Bembows' and Ettenwater's future together, weirdly and wonderfully intertwined.

Mr Seathwaite stiffened.

'Now's the moment, youth. Hold on to your hat.'

Suddenly the Bembow logo shone out over the water in a great arch of fizzing light: a gambolling child holding hands with a couple of dancing parents and WHAT YOU WANT TO DO-IO inscribed in incandescent script underneath.

Salvoes of rockets accompanied this portent.

Underneath the arch, the lake sent forth myriad reflections while the surrounding hills echoed back their quotient of pops and bangs.

Something from *The Prelude* came to Freddie's mind – skating, exulting, leaving the throng, echoing hills, yes, 'cutting across the reflex of a star', that was it – and here there were a thousand stars multiplying and colliding in the shining water as the breeze stirred the surface.

Stars, indeed. But no monster. The water remained obstinately empty.

Freddie's mind spun like a Catherine wheel. It wasn't going to happen. The gas hadn't inflated. There was a leak. The thing had perished.

Whatever the reason, there was going to be a frost on a more than Wordsworthian scale. Even now the last lights of the arch were igniting. Soon the effect would begin to fade. What would the Bembows say to only half a set piece?

The spectators, pleased with the general effect, but somehow expecting more, were already restless. Freddie consulted his watch. The monster was three minutes late.

'It's not working . . .' he said unnecessarily to Mr Seathwaite, who was grabbing his shoulder so hard it hurt.

He tried not to sound relieved.

'It will work,' said Mr Seathwaite. 'It must work. Uncle Gussie was a Sapper.'

Looking round, Freddie saw Mrs Seathwaite and Bertrand standing close behind them. He gave her a sickly apologetic grin.

Even as he turned, however, he heard a sudden shout

from one of the spectators by the water, followed by a low animal murmur of interest from the crowd.

He looked again and saw . . . could it be?. . . yes, there was a definite blackness in the water . . . a stirring . . . a snout . . . eyes . . . long flat prehistoric head.

The crowd went mad.

True, a few pulled back, alarmed. One or two children hid their faces in their mothers' skirts. A couple of greybeards started legging it back towards the bar. But the majority were enraptured. Cheers and huzzahs mingled with wild calls from the first and second cornets.

The crowd held its breath again. More and more of the monster was emerging. One . . . two . . . three great humps appeared.

The applause was like the braying of a great beast itself as the illuminated arch burned on, revealing the full glory of the creature. The local photographers flashed away like a Roman candelabra.

Leacock was trying to make himself heard.

'Thank you, thank you . . .'

It was Bembows' day. Freddie stole a glance at Mr Seathwaite. He was like a man who has just seen his son receive the Sword of Honour at Sandhurst, or his daughter dance Odette/Odile at the Royal Opera House. All his hopes were fulfilled, all his wishes come true.

Time itself seemed to falter and stop.

And then there was another noise from the crowd. One of fascination, yes, but doubt this time as well. For the monster was still coming, growing bigger, drawing nearer, looking like a deranged dirigible.

Some of the more impressionable now started to run, but most remained rooted to the spot.

'What the . . .' began Mr Seathwaite, a terrible doubt beginning to tinge his moment of triumph.

Freddie stole a glance at Mrs Seathwaite. She looked at

him meaningfully as if to say: 'Well done.' Mr Seathwaite intercepted the exchange.

'No,' he cried, running to the water's edge.

'Stop him,' shouted someone.

The monster was swelling nightmarishly, towering above them like Nemesis.

'The valve,' shouted Mr Seathwaite, manically, 'they've stuck the bloody valve. Let me go, you fools. I must get to the valve.'

He was floundering about in the water with three men holding him back. The monster, big as a hillock now, loomed over them sausage-tight and prodigious. Indeed, it began to be almost airborne as its inner tubing expanded far past all possible tolerance.

It started to bob and bounce, smacking the water, making a horrible animal-like hungry noise.

Freddie, consumed with guilt at the role he had played in this public humiliation for Mr Seathwaite, spotted the reprobate ex-vicar down on his knees.

'The sign,' he was crying, 'it is the sign.'

Others joined him in earnest prayer.

It was impossible for the remainder of the crowd now to do anything but stand and watch.

'Too late. Get back!' yelled Mr Seathwaite, knowing only too well what lay inside his creation.

For Freddie it was like the inevitable climax of a Greek tragedy – a phenomenon often referred to in literature lessons by Gibbers but never experienced so poignantly in real life – impossible to forestall, a terrible justice in its implacable unfolding.

It was Mrs Seathwaite's turn to hog the laurels.

She stood with the beautiful youth beside her, like a triumphant Deianeira while her husband writhed in the poisoned shirt of Nessus.

Who could tell what Bertrand was thinking? It was his

fortune that his beautiful face registered nothing but beauty. It was a mask, a statue that gave nothing away. Had Mrs Seathwaite told him how she had despatched Freddie down to the boathouse, two mornings ago when her husband lay in sottish sleep, to secure Ettie's valve with chewing gum, cork, champagne wire and sealing wax? He gave no sign.

There was a long pause. Time slowed again, pendulous as a plesiosaur.

Suddenly the monster exploded.

A vast and unconceivably horrible cloud of stench and matter filled the air. Skin, offal, rancid fat, fish, rotting vegetation, foul fruit, carcasses small and large in various stages of dismembership skidded and ricocheted like squibs. Part of a duck's foot hit Freddie sharply on the cheek. Every corner of the field had its own register of putrid affront.

It was some balm to Freddie – even in the midst of his guilt and shame – to see that the VIPs' podium appeared to have suffered a direct hit. He could see the Bembows wiping each other with some bunting. The bearer of the Mayor's chain lay recumbent, felled by a suppurating vegetable marrow, and a rural district counsellor was sitting dazedly trying to extricate himself from a string of blue intestine that had wound round his neck like a python . . .

A skull of some kind, of uncertain age and origin, rocked about on the grass in a bizarre semblance of mirth.

Mrs Seathwaite spotted it and screamed, 'Jojo.'

She made vague cradling motions with her hands.

Freddie wondered whether Mr Seathwaite really had dredged up the death's head. He could hardly blame the man for elasticity with the truth when he himself had practised such deceit.

He looked round for Mr Seathwaite but he seemed to

have disappeared in the mêlée. Freddie could not actually see anyone being lynched, but from the temper of the spectators you could sense it was on the cards. He hoped he wasn't going to have to reveal his part in the disaster in order to save Mr Seathwaite from being strung up. He would do it, of course. The way he felt now, in fact, he had half a mind to jump in the lake and call the whole thing a day.

As he mooched his way from the field – not all that slowly: the smell was enough to call the vultures from the Sahara – there was only one comfort. The evening's work had not advanced the cause of Leacock and the Bembows.

Somewhere in the distance, the band had rallied and, in the spirit of the *Titanic*, were bravely playing hymns as the occasion slid downhill.

Freddie detected 'Eternal Father, Strong to Save', music by the great John Bacchus, before he crossed the little bridge and the strains were blotted out by the scurrying arpeggios of the stream.

43

As he approached Flat Foot, his feelings of waste and melancholy increased, urged on by a sense of anticlimax and a strong smell of bad duck on his shirt collar.

The whole holiday which had looked so bleak on arrival and which had provided so many troughs and up-turns was almost at an end. The manifestation of Ettenwater's own monster, which was to have provided the highest point of all, had turned inconceivably sour. He didn't want to go home. He couldn't stay. He didn't even want to wank. He was no use to man or woman, and he didn't even want himself.

He lay on his bed in the gathering darkness and snivelled. Snivelling, maybe, he thought; but tosser, no.

He became aware of someone knocking at the door.

'Come in,' he said hopelessly.

It was Mrs Aylott.

'Is that you?' she asked.

'Yes,' he sniffed.

'All in the dark?'

She advanced and peered at him.

'Yes.'

'No wonder you've got such a long face. Come into the kitchen and I'll make you some tea.'

Miraculously, she seemed to have escaped the vile deluge. She looked as fresh and pretty as she had when he met her earlier – fresher, because she was smelling of something nice.

'I didn't like the look of that thing,' she said, 'so I stood well clear.'

'I'm afraid it was my fault,' said Freddie.

He told her about it. It was nice to get it off his chest.

As he concluded his story, his depression returned. It really was a despicable thing for him to have done. Apart from anything else, the monster was virtually irreplaceable. He had traduced the very name of monster where it should be most respected. If the Greeks were anything to go by, there would be retribution.

He lifted his head and found that she was laughing.

'It's no joke for me,' he said. 'I let everyone down except Mrs Seathwaite, and I think she's evil.'

It made her laugh all the more.

He was offended.

'Well, if all you can do is laugh,' he said huffily, 'I think I'll go back to my room if you don't mind.'

'Don't go,' she said placatingly, reaching out and touching his hand, 'I like to laugh. I haven't had much to laugh about lately. Have a chocolate biscuit and tell me about the rest of your holiday.'

So he told her about Bertrand, and Hell Hall, and the Seathwaites, and Bertrand and Diana and Elizabeth, and how he felt such a failure, and no one wanted him, and he didn't want to go home; and suddenly he was kissing her because she had bent down to bring her face close to his, and his hands were stroking her dress and unbuttoning the shirt-waister top and she was letting him slip his hands into the prefectly privacy of her bra, and he didn't stop for a moment to think of how Aitken said you should do it.

'Come upstairs, darling,' said Mrs Aylott. 'It'll be better there, won't it? Yes?'

44

Freddie was lying beside Mrs Aylott, looking at her breasts, and thinking, and not thinking while she settled herself on the pillow and smoked a cigarette.

It was the happiest moment of his life.

On second thoughts, he wasn't so keen on the cigarette. It spoke of something less than rapture. He mentioned it to her.

'You know what they say,' she said. '"Whatever the pleasure. Player's complete it."'

She stretched like the young bride in the picture Farty Arty Phillpotts was always banging on about in *The Rake's Progress*; 'feline, indolent and luxurious', said Farty.

Freddie thought he would never love anyone so much as Mrs Aylott. He suddenly remembered something.

'Oh gosh. I didn't put a you-know-what on.'

'A you-know?'

'Thing.'

'Thing?'

'French letter sort of thing. I only have one and I think it's sort of perished.'

'Don't worry,' she said. 'You don't have to worry about that.'

'I can't go back, you know,' he told her. 'I want to stay with you always.'

There was a step outside on the stairs.

'Oh my God,' she said. 'Who the hell's that?'

She drew the bedclothes around her and sat up. Freddie scrambled into his Aertex pants and tried to get under the bed.

'Well, well, well,' said Mr Leacock, 'what have we here? When the cat's away, the vice will play? Is that it, young 'un? Dirty little man. Thought I'd find you here.'

'Get out of my bedroom,' said Mrs Aylott. 'In fact, get out of my house. Know how you smell? You smell terrible.'

'Ah, but it's not your house, is it, Missus? Or it won't be soon.'

'You know what the Clause says.'

'I know what the Clause says.'

'What does the Clause say?' asked Freddie, since everyone else seemed to know.

'The Clause says,' said Mrs Aylott, 'that if I become pregnant within forty days of last Friday, we have the option of cancelling the sale.'

Even Freddie, who knew little about such matters, thought it was an unusual clause.

'Why did you want the Clause?' he asked.

'Simple,' she said. 'I told Aylott the only way I'd stay here was if we had a family. It's too lonely otherwise. So when he,' nodding at Leacock, 'lent us money and then wanted it back double quick, we had no option but to agree to sell to him.'

'Fair price, Missus, fair price.'

'It would've been if there'd been no coercion.'

'Coercion is the lubrication of commerce, Missus.'

'Coercion made me want to put the Clause in. Leacock didn't mind. Humour a woman, it's meat and drink to 'em. That's what he said. There's none so queer as folk unless it's women. He'd done his research. He knew that Aylott can't have children because of his mumps. Aylott doesn't know that, but he knew that. But one thing he didn't think about was what the Clause didn't say.'

'All right, then,' said Leacock, looking slightly discomfited, 'what didn't the Clause say?'

'It didn't say that I had to have children by Mr Aylott.'

'Oooh. Why . . . you dirty woman,' said Mr Leacock. 'That's evil, that is. Like a brood mare.'

'Yes,' said Mrs Aylott, happily. 'And I've got a bet on with the bookie too. I showed him all the stuff from the hospital, making out it was my fault we couldn't have children. They say it's psychologically bad for a man, you know. Of course, I had to tell Aylott later. Any road, the bookie gave me twenty to one against. So if I have a baby, I get the money to pay you off. And then we can start on this notion I've got about converting the goat-house and making a holiday hamlet here. It's one of the things Aylott's talking to his accountant about . . . What have you got to say to that, Cleverclogs?'

'You evil woman,' repeated Leacock, thoroughly mortified.

A terrible thought had been consuming all Freddie's happiness while this exchange went on. He now turned to Mrs Aylott, ashen-faced.

'You don't mean . . . you . . . no . . .'

She looked at him impatiently.

'What is it?'

'You don't mean you just wanted to go to bed with me so you could have a . . . baby . . .'

The word was too horrible almost to say. He was too young to have a baby. Fathering a child, it was well known at school, was the most ghastly thing that could possibly happen.

'That's about the long and short of it, young 'un,' said Leacock malodorously. 'You were taken for a stud, that's what you were.'

'Oh,' cried Freddie.

'Wait till I tell your husband about your goings on. It's shameless. With a young lad too.'

'You never went with a young girl?'

'Well, I . . . that's different.'

'Anyway,' continued Mrs Aylott, 'my husband knows. He knew about the French lad too. Actually, he suggested it.'

There were no words that could express Freddie's feelings. He had had too many emotions for one day.

'Don't take on so, Freddie. You had a nice time. I really feel you may have done the trick. Don't you want me to have your baby?'

'Ugh,' cried Freddie, and ran from the room forgetting that his shoes weren't done up and falling down the stairs.

'In for a penny, in for a pound,' he heard Mr Leacock say, as he gathered himself up.

He had the distinct impression that Leacock was going to take his trousers off.

In his room again, Freddie couldn't cry. He had slept with a real woman, whatever the circumstances, so it proved he was grown up. Grownups didn't blub. At least men didn't anyway.

The only adult thing to do was to get drunk. Rummaging in the tallboy, he found Bertrand's half-empty bottle of brandy. He poured some of it into a toothbrush tumbler, and swigged. It tasted of Euthymol but it seemed to chase out the clammy toad that had taken up residence in his belly. He gasped down the first mugful and chased it with a second.

When Bertrand returned, he was drunk.

'"Wisdom and spirit of the Universe,"' he declaimed, waving the Martell bottle, and suddenly throwing up on the floor.

Bertrand tidied him, and put him to bed.

'A most interesting vacation, Freddie. Next year you must come to France.'

45

It was his first hangover, but he knew what it was. It was the father and mother of one.

No, he thought, as he clambered painfully into consciousness, with that ponderous woody sensation in the brain that is the mark of a really serious affront; no, it is the stepfather and mother of a hangover.

That was quite enough thinking for a bit. But there was something else his brain was trying to tell him. What? Sorry? Ahhh. His stepfather and mother would be arriving this morning. Pincers gouged his temples as he grappled with the thought. Rollo? He couldn't face Rollo today. Rollo was bad enough when you were feeling well.

He rolled his log of a head over and looked at his watch for a minute or two before it began to tell him the time.

It was a quarter to nine. They were going to be late for breakfast.

He scrabbled vainly at the sheet and lay down again moaning. He would never be fit for the car at noon, let alone breakfast. They must leave him here to die.

Bertrand gave him more water, and drew the curtains a little. Freddie shrank back, groaning horribly, like Dracula caught out of the coffin. Bertrand pulled the curtain back again, dressed in the darkened room, and padded off up the corridor.

Presently Mrs Aylott came in with some tea and toast.

'Eat,' she said. 'You'll feel better by and by.'

'Are you really going to have a baby?'

''Course I am.'

'Ohhhh.'

But the pain in his head shut out all else. She put a cool hand on his brow and left the room.

Presently, after sipping a little tea and nibbling a little toast, he fell asleep again.

He woke to find Bertrand in the room, packing. His headache had almost gone. It was eleven o'clock.

'I feel better,' he said. 'I'd better finish packing. They'll be here in an hour. Don't tell them I've been like this, will you?'

'Mummy's the word.'

'Don't tell them anything.'

He thought of something else he wanted to say.

'You didn't . . . you know . . . with Mr and Mrs Seathwaite, did you?'

'What do you think?'

By twelve, their cases were in the hall. At ten past twelve, the black Triumph with Rollo at the wheel swung into the drive and halted at the front door, spraying gravel around. His mother emerged, optimistic and tweedy.

'Hullo, darling.'

She gave him a kiss. He felt ridiculously shy.

'Hullo, Bertrand.'

'Bonjour, Madame.'

'Did you have a nice time?'

'Yes, thank you. Very nice.'

'There you are. It wasn't so bad after all.'

Mrs Aylott appeared, smoothing her hair.

'There's nice Mrs Aylott. I hope they weren't too much trouble.'

'Not at all. They were no trouble at all.'

'Thank you so much for having them.'

Mrs Aylott smiled bountifully.

'It was a pleasure,' she said.

The cases were loaded, the bill paid, the goodbyes exchanged and messages relayed for Isobel and Mr

267

Aylott. The boys piled into the car, and Rollo chewed up the gravel again.

As they swung out through the gates, it started to rain.

Freddie sat in silence as the tyres swished, the windscreen wiper made its little moan, and his mother chatted brightly to Bertrand.

'Frap?'

Freddie knew this would happen.

'Yes,' he answered, flatly.

The little white hairs on Rollo's neck had grown longer and fluffier in the last fortnight.

'You're very quiet, Frap. Missing the goooooooaaaaats?' he bleated.

Rollo would never leave an old joke unsqueezed if a drop more juice could be got out of it.

'Oh, why don't you shut up?' said Freddie.

'Freddie,' exclaimed his mother, shocked.

It was the first time he had ever voiced direct dislike at his stepfather.

Freddie's mother knew that Rollo wasn't the ideal father substitute, but he was fond of her and he paid the bills and what was one to do? So she applied herself to keeping the peace, which usually meant Freddie having to keep his mouth shut.

Bertrand grinned at him round the corner of a tennis racket press.

Rollo's neck, under the fringe of fluffy white hairs, flushed but he said nothing.

Freddie wondered whether Hildegard would have shaved her armpits when they got back. Perhaps it was time he bought some new French letters.

They rounded a bend.

'Look, boys,' said Freddie's mother, glad to change the subject, 'one last view of the lake.'

There it was, just a fraction of a glimpse of the western shore, folded between trees and hills.

'Oh. It's coming back,' said his mother suddenly. 'Of course.'

'What's coming back?'

He half turned in case it was a monster, or *Proserpine*.

'That story of Cousin Percy . . . you know, Percy the Archaeologist.'

'Perky the Arseologist,' said Rollo.

'He met this man who'd been invalided up to the Seathwaites. A Free Frenchman, he was, apparently. Nice chap. A bit eccentric, you know . . . Gallic. Well, he said he suddenly felt he just had to leave. So he took the milk train early one morning and tooled straight back to London without saying a word.'

'Bad show,' said Rollo.

'Apparently he felt quite bad about it, but he simply couldn't take the climate. I think that's what he said. He suddenly couldn't take it any more.'

'He couldn't take it,' crowed Rollo. 'Couldn't . . . taaake it.'

'Funny, wasn't it?'

'Rude.'

'Very.'

'But that's the French for you.'

'Ssh, Rollo. The French can have lovely manners. Can't they, Bertrand?'

'Bien sûr. Toujours la politesse.'

Freddie gave a little sigh and looked at Bertrand, who smiled and shrugged. So that was the truth about Jojo. He simply did a bunk.

He wondered what Mr Seathwaite would be doing today. He thought of Hell Hall; so orderly, so loveless. He thought of his child nestling in Mrs Aylott's comfortable uterus.

He turned his head away.

269

'"And when the deed was done,
I heard among the solitary hills
Low breathings coming after me
And sounds of indistinguishable motion,"'

he said.
'What's that? Freddie,' asked his mother.
   'That?' he said. 'Oh that. Only Wordsworth.'

Epilogue

The Bembows Holiday Hamlets development at Etten-water never took place.

The monster incident had not helped foster enthusiasm among either the locals or their rural district counsellors, as Mrs Seathwaite had foreseen; but it was Leacock's samples of rocks and stones and trees that did the trick.

Bembows left nothing to chance, and it was part of their policy to research the locality thoroughly before any kind of implementation.

Their solicitors had noted the Government Research Station at Ettenmouth, and just in time had discovered it was a plutonium reprocessing plant.

Though less was publicly known about such places at the time, there was already some disquiet in certain quarters, and there had been mishaps reported. (The fire engines noted by Mr Seathwaite had been going to just such an incident.) Leacock had been instructed to collect samples, and these, on investigation, proved to contain significant traces of radioactivity – emanating from just those towers that Freddie and Bertrand had seen on their conquest of Stickletop.

Two years later, there was more than just an incident. One of the piles actually caught fire, and a radioactive cloud dragoned out and spread across Northern England and Europe. It was all kept very quiet, but the Bembows heard about it and congratulated themselves.

Leacock was made a director.

Freddie got his A Levels and, an unexpected bonus, a

State Scholarship on the strength of his Wordsworth paper.

Bertrand was killed in a car crash during National Service in Algeria.

Mr and Mrs Seathwaite continued their mutual antagonism on the shores of Ettenwater until well into their seventies.

Isobel went back to the United States and later re-surfaced as a doyenne of pop culture.

Jackie continued to live in his cottage and ply his boats.

And Mr and Mrs Aylott did indeed become the proud parents of a little boy. They sold the goats and turned the sheds into chalets. They became, in fact, quite prosperous. Their child later developed leukaemia.

Freddie never knew about the child – his birth or his death.

Rollo lived till he was ninety, just to thwart Freddie's prayers. Freddie's mother lives energetically on.

Or perhaps it isn't like that at all. All things are possible in disordering Time.

The Second Law of Thermodynamics suggests – as does Wordsworth – that things only get worse, so it seems reasonable to put a filter tinged with pessimism over any subsequent histories; but not too much because it doesn't do to mope.

On one issue at least it is possible to give an unambiguous report.

Ettenwater today looks much as it did thirty years ago. The scree still stands poised, halted in its course by the almighty command which has not yet been rescinded. The wind still chafes the flood. And stalky flotsam still froths at the edge with only a minor admixture of plastic bags and cola cans; for development has been limited.

The place, after all, still has its monster.